THE GARDENE
HANDBO

THE GARDENERS' WORLD HANDBOOK

PRACTICAL ADVICE FROM BBC TV's GARDENERS' WORLD EXPERTS

EDITED BY
JOHN KENYON & PHIL FRANKLIN

BBC BOOKS

Published by BBC Books
A division of BBC Enterprises Ltd
Woodlands, 80 Wood Lane
London W12 0TT

First published 1988

ISBN 0 563 20627 6

Typeset in 10/12pt Sabon,
printed and bound in Great Britain by
Redwood Burn Limited, Trowbridge, Wiltshire

CONTENTS

AVERAGE LAST FROSTS

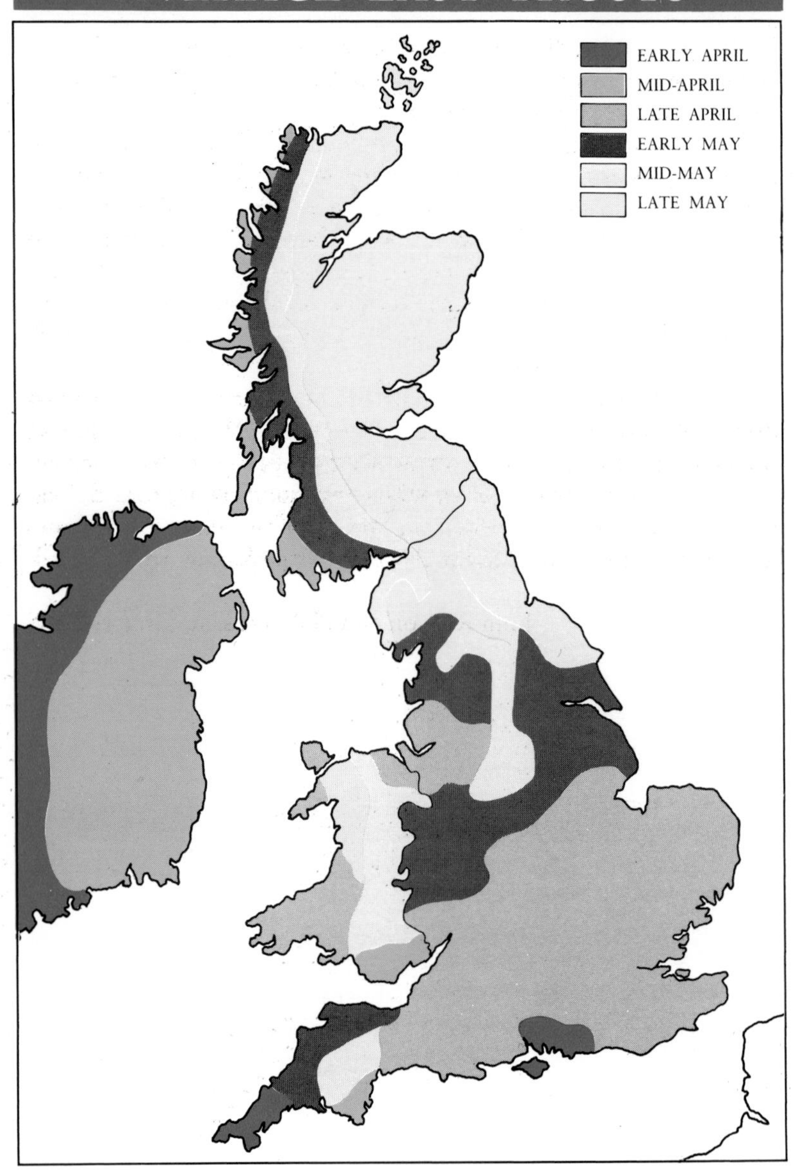

This is based on information provided by the Meteorological Office *but* they point out that, due to the vagaries of our island climate, it is reliable for only four years out of five. They don't specify which four years. Remember also that if your garden is above 400ft (122m), the chances of late frosts in spring increase greatly.

PREFACE

This book aims to fill a void in publications on gardening which is manifest to us from the thousands of letters that are sent to the *Gardeners' World* office every year.

Like the programme it has a lot of ideas and timely advice on how to make your garden work for you, growing good things to eat and splendid plants to look at. Like the television presentations it does not pretend to give you an A to Z plan for the perfect garden, but attempts to be a catalyst to fire up your gardening enthusiasm. One word of warning: although we allocate garden tasks to particular months of the year, the timetable will vary according to the area of the country in which you live (see map on page 6).

This handbook does what the programme cannot do, and what other books do not do, and that is give you an enormous range of sources from which to find out answers to problems for yourself. Someone in our lists can provide a blueprint for growing rare alpines, or organic cabbages, and there is the address of the nursery that grows the shrub that they didn't have in the fourteen garden centres you tried.

John Kenyon and Phil Franklin, January 1988

LIST OF CONTRIBUTORS

Alan Bloom founded Bressingham Gardens, near Diss in Norfolk, now one of the biggest nurseries in the United Kingdom. There are a hundred and more wonderful garden plants that we can buy and grow that, without his enthusiasm and careful selection, would still be unobtainable.

Dr Stefan Buczacki is a stalwart of the *Gardeners' Question Time* team on Radio 4, and appears regularly on *Gardeners' World*. His scientific background qualifies him in all things botanical, especially gardeners' problems. Through his books and broadcasts he likes to emphasise the whys as well as the hows.

Geoff Hamilton presents *Gardeners' World* nearly every week and his garden at Barnsdale is featured at least once a month throughout the year. Trained at Writtle Agricultural College, he started in landscaping and journalism, becoming editor of *Practical Gardening* magazine, from which he resigned to build up his 'television' garden and write books and articles on nearly every facet of gardening.

Clay Jones is chairman of Radio 4's *Gardeners' Question Time* and frequently presents *Gardeners' World*. The instructions on those seed packets that you buy may very often be his, for he has been a gardening journalist for more years than he will admit to. He boasts that he is winning the battle on an acre of ground overlooking the Severn Estuary, where he is already growing just about everything.

John Kelly is a regular presenter of *Gardeners' World*. He is curator of Abbotsbury Gardens, near Weymouth, Dorset, the nearest we have in Britain to the sub-tropical, where he looks after a lot of tender plants from abroad and has to make sure that he always has replacements if our climate kills them off: hence his expertise at taking cuttings. Paradoxically his great love is for those plants from the cold high mountains – the alpines.

Roy Lancaster started exploring the world of plants on rubbish tips near Bolton in Lancashire when just a small boy. During National Service in Malaya he tangled with the jungle, and got hooked on plant collecting and identification. He has been at it ever since. Whilst at Hilliers he became part-author of the definitive work on trees and shrubs, and his books, articles, lectures and broadcasts have established him as a world authority on all that delights us in gardens.

Ashley Stephenson is Bailiff of the Royal Parks. He was born not too far from 'Capability' Brown's birthplace and, like Brown, his gardening education was at the sharp end. In the very different circumstances of the twentieth century, he has made his own impact, particularly in the Royal Parks.

Anne Swithinbank is a regular presenter of *Gardeners' World*. Much of her expertise was gained in the Royal Horticultural Society Gardens at Wisley, where she worked for five years. She is now a garden consultant, the sort that rolls up sleeves and digs up weeds as well as providing advice.

SPRING

FEBRUARY
MARCH
APRIL

WHY NOT GROW SOMETHING DIFFERENT?
Roy Lancaster

ALPINES
John Kelly

PLANT FOODS AND PLANT FEEDING
Stefan Buczacki

FEBRUARY

VEGETABLE PATCH

The only real joy this month is in harvesting and eating any winter vegetables still in the ground or above it. Brussels sprouts and purple sprouting broccoli are wonderful, but they take up a lot of space for a good part of the year.

A home-made cloche

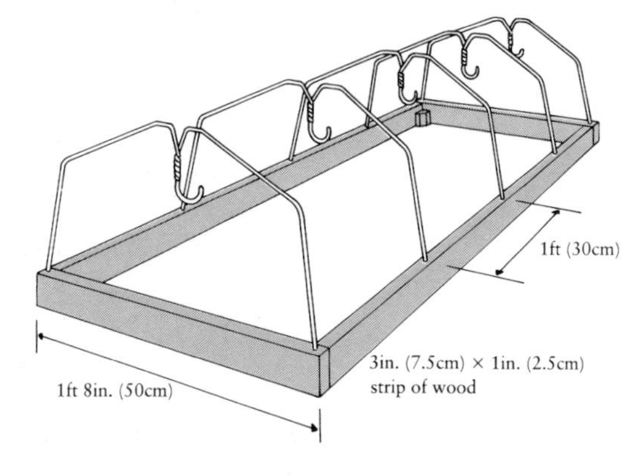

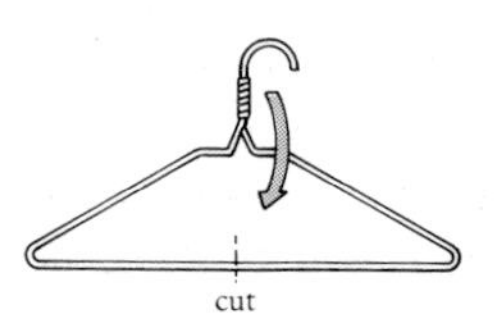

Bend hook down

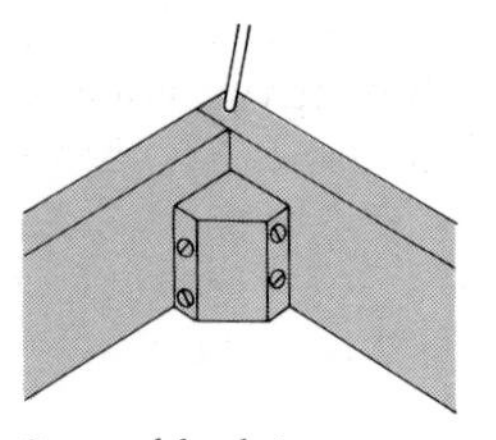

Screw block into corner

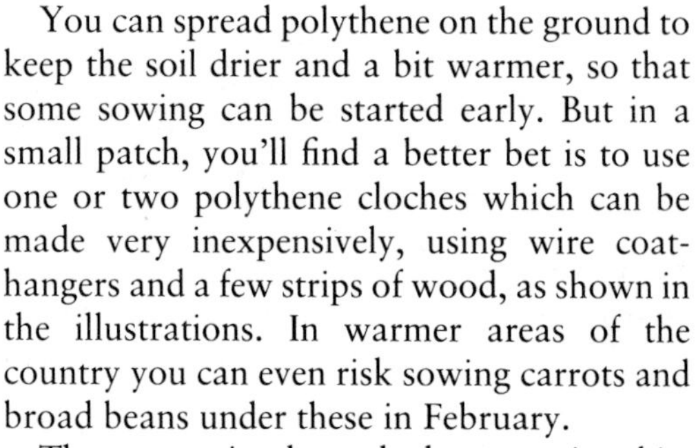

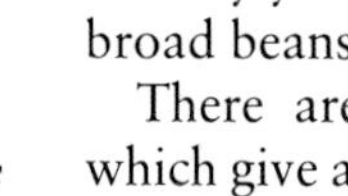

Fold plastic and secure with drawing pins

You can spread polythene on the ground to keep the soil drier and a bit warmer, so that some sowing can be started early. But in a small patch, you'll find a better bet is to use one or two polythene cloches which can be made very inexpensively, using wire coat-hangers and a few strips of wood, as shown in the illustrations. In warmer areas of the country you can even risk sowing carrots and broad beans under these in February.

There are simple and cheap testing kits which give an indication of the acidity of your soil. Most vegetables, especially brassicas (the

HOW MUCH IS A HANDFUL?

A handful (of fertiliser, grass seed, etc.) is such a variable amount that it is best to forget it and make yourself a simple measure. Weigh 1oz (25g), 2oz (50g), 3oz (75g), 4oz (100g) and 5oz (125g) into a yoghurt carton or similar container and mark the side in each case. Most advice given on packets is in ounces per square yard/grams per square metre.

cabbage family), do not like acid soils, and two or three handfuls of lime to the square yard where you plan to plant them will help to minimise clubroot, that awful disease that either kills or maims them and which thrives in acid soil. (See page 39 for how to calculate the correct amount of lime for your particular soil.)

If you have not finished digging and clearing up, do it now.

LAWN

If your aim is to have the perfect surface for clock golf, croquet or bowls, spike the lawn all over with a fork, then put on fertilisers. For the rest of us it is a good idea to spike the wet bits, particularly where puddles form; otherwise ignore the lawn this month.

February is a good month to lay turf, to give it time to bed in before the grass starts to grow. (See page 12 for how to calculate the amount of turf you need.) Buying turf is a hazardous venture, however, and it is not cheap, so be sure that it is good before you are committed to a purchase. If you are worried about it, why not wait till the soil has warmed up and sow seed instead?

FLOWER BEDS & BORDERS

This is a very good time to look over the hedges of neighbours who have the sort of garden you would like. They will have spring bulbs in flower – not just snowdrops and crocuses, but cyclamen, aconites, scillas and irises. Get out the catalogues and make a note on your garden plan of the ones you like best. Bulbs are the least demanding of plants: everyone should have some. When snowdrops have finished flowering, any big clumps can be lifted, divided, and replanted now.

Cleanliness is next to Godliness, so clean up weeds, leaves and all things that might harbour disease and pests. Those devils, slugs, can be hammered by the non-organic gardener with pellets or, better still, liquid killers which cannot harm pets and wildlife. They are probably everywhere, but damp, shady places are favourite.

HOUSEPLANTS, WINDOW BOXES, TUBS & TROUGHS

Outside, the well organised have tubs and boxes full of bulbs in flower. The rest of us think about summer, and containers of any sort need cleaning. Granny did her wooden window boxes by brushing around a liberal amount of paraffin inside, then setting it on fire. She painted them outside. Year after year after year, she grew wonderful disease-free plants.

Indoors, especially where they have to live with central heating, houseplants need humidity and very little else (see page 105).

FRUIT TREES & BUSHES

If you have been thinking that your fruit trees and bushes need a tar oil wash but haven't done it yet, take a very good look at them. If the buds have started to swell, *do not do it*, because it is strong stuff and might damage them.

Spray grass and weeds, which grow over the roots and compete for plant food, with a dilute dose of Weedex (see packet); organic converts will remove them by their own physical efforts.

If you have no raspberries, it is not too late to buy a few canes and plant them. They yield well, eat well and freeze well, and don't take up too much ground. Autumn-fruiting raspberries should be cut down now to within 2 or 3in. (5–7.5cm) of the ground.

Strawberries should be covered with cloches for an early crop.

HOW MUCH TURF DO I BUY?

Turf is usually sold in strips 1yd (1m) long by 1ft (30cm) wide, so the calculation is simple. Find out how many square yards/metres you have to cover and multiply by three. That will give you the number of turves you require.

WINDOWSILL, COLD FRAME & GREENHOUSE

Check those seed packets – a great many seeds can be sown in February. Germinate them on the top shelf of the airing cupboard and, as soon as the shoots appear, transfer them to the windowsill.

Don't get too enthusiastic, however: remember that you will have to nurture the small plants for a long time before they can be put out in the garden, so don't grow more than you have room for indoors. They require plenty of light and protection from frost. Tomatoes in particular need an early start, and in small pots they don't take up much room.

Mildew often appears under glass at this time of year. The old-fashioned remedy is to spray with a solution of potassium sulphide at 1oz (25g) to 3 gallons (13.5 litres) of water (about ⅔oz to a bucket).

TREES, SHRUBS & CLIMBERS

If you have any plans to plant new bare-rooted specimens (which are cheaper than container-grown ones), this is your last chance. Don't be too anxious to prune – you will do a better job when you can see buds beginning to swell: they show where to cut back to.

GENERAL

As the weather is usually at its worst, and nearly everything is hibernating, doing nothing at all should not be regarded as a sin.

MARCH

VEGETABLE PATCH

As our winters seem to spread later and later into the year, it is sensible not to rush into sowing too many seeds. In the south, if those home-made cloches have been covering the ground for the last month, leeks, carrots, beetroot and, of course, early potatoes (which have first been chitted – see below) can go in underneath them, but remember that the early seedling catches the frost. In the north you'll have to pin down your cloches or polythene so the March winds don't blow them away.

Optimists will have a go with everything. The cost of a third of a packet of seeds will not break the bank. They sow them, and if the seedlings get nipped, they sow some more.

Onion sets and shallots do much better with an early start, but they are more expensive than seed.

When sowing vegetable or flower seeds, use a line. It helps differentiate between the tiny plants you want to grow, and the weeds that germinate at the same time. It also makes subsequent hoeing easy and looks better.

Don't sow too deeply. Between ¼ and ½in. (6–13mm) is the maximum for most seeds, with the exception of beans, peas and potatoes. Try to break up the soil into which you intend to sow the seed as finely as possible. Then the seed will be sown at an even depth, the soil particles will retain moisture round it, and the roots make immediate contact with moisture and food.

CHITTING

As soon as a shoot or root appars, a seed has chitted – that is, started in growth. The term is most often applied to seed potatoes, which are placed in a box with the eyes upwards. Because the shoots begin to grow in the light, they are short and tough, and don't get knocked off at planting time. In the dark, they grow long, white and fragile.

LAWN

If the grass is doing nothing, you can do the same. If it is starting to grow, mow it with the blades set high.

If you are keen to have the perfect velvet lawn, you can buy combined fertilisers and moss killers, though these work best when growing has started in earnest. Alternatively, try the moss killer mixture described below. A good raking sets the grass up for the first mowing, gets a bit of air to the soil and removes dead material.

FLOWER BEDS & BORDERS

Southerners and the brave sow hardy annuals in late March.

Two or 3oz of Growmore per square yard (50–75g per square metre) raked in everywhere will provide food for plants already growing, and for this year's seedlings. If you are an organic enthusiast, you will probably prefer to use blood, fish and bonemeal.

In balmy climes roses can be pruned now, and it is true that early blooms follow early pruning. However, it is safer to wait until the buds on the main stems begin to swell naturally – they grow into the branches that bear the flowers. Early pruning stimulates their growth, and late frosts kill them off. Some fertiliser, applied as above, and then a good mulch will encourage early growth.

Weeds are easily dealt with by hoeing when they are small, a weekly task from now until October. Be careful not to knock off the new shoots of perennials that may be starting to grow.

A bed of fine soil newly sown with seed will

CHEAP MOSS CONTROL

Fine silver sand	20 parts by weight
Sulphate of ammonia	3 parts by weight
Sulphate of iron	1 part by weight

Mix well and apply at a rate of 4oz per square yard (100g per square metre) during spring and summer.

attract cats like a candle does moths. There is no more frustrating sight than next door's tom scratching out your tiny seedlings. Wire netting or twigs are more effective and cheaper than proprietary cat-repelling compounds.

Remove dead flowers and seed pods from crocuses and daffodils so that they put their energy back into the bulb.

HOUSEPLANTS, WINDOW BOXES, TUBS & TROUGHS

Plants that have outgrown their pots should be potted on. Check first to see if they are getting root bound by knocking them out of the pot. Unless there is a mass of root, put them back and leave them alone. If they need a bigger pot, one size larger is enough.

All your plants will benefit from a liquid feed at this time of year.

Take cuttings from new growth on fuchsias and geraniums. Remember that geraniums do not need rooting power: they strike better without.

It should be safe to sow hardy annuals in containers now because it is easy to protect them by placing glass or polythene over the top. Check frequently to make sure that they don't get dry.

Instead of flowers you could sow some herbs. Go and have a look at seed packets in the garden centre.

Potting on a rootbound plant

a

b

c

FRUIT TREES & BUSHES

You can still prune to tidy up trees to make a good open structure that will let in air and light. Rising sap reduces the risk of infection to the cut. However you would still be well advised to cover it with wound paint for extra protection.

Spray apples and pears against scab, and cane fruits against spot and spur blight. Benlate does both jobs.

Peaches and nectarines growing up walls flower early. Old lace or net curtains draped over the trees will protect against frost, but be careful not to damage the flowers when positioning these.

Some fertiliser spread over the root area and covered with a mulch is good news for all trees and bushes. Lime should not be used unless you know the tree or bush likes an alkaline soil.

WINDOWSILL, COLD FRAME & GREENHOUSE

Sweet peas, which are fairly tough, can be hardened off now. That means transferring the small plants from the windowsill inside to a cold frame outside. A piece of old carpet over the top on very cold nights will protect from hard frost.

If airing cupboard and windowsill space allows, sow half-hardy annuals. Nemesia, petunias, candytuft and antirrhinums are a must. Sow thinly in boxes and don't bother to thin the seedlings: it's tiresome and time-consuming. Of course, if you see no necessity to be ahead of the game, wait a bit and sow them outside directly into the soil.

Dahlia tubers should be placed in moist compost and wrapped thickly in newspaper to keep out frost. Keep an eye on them: when the shoots start to grow, they must then have light. Wrap them up again on frosty nights. If you are greedy, you can cut them up provided there is some tuber (fat root) attached to each bud.

TREES, SHRUBS & CLIMBERS

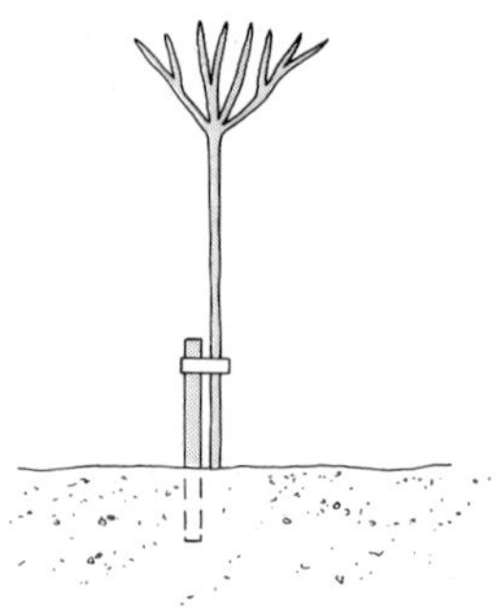

Staking a young tree

Windy weather will show up any bad staking on young trees. The stake need be no more than 1ft (30cm) above ground level, as shown in the illustration. Check the ties regularly.

Get to know your shrubs. Some, like buddleia and hydrangea, need cutting right down to low buds; others need pruning after flowering; others you prune at your peril, or certainly theirs.

If you collected seeds from shrubs like broom or cotoneaster in the autumn, sow now in the cold frame in sandy soil. Make sure that they don't dry out. As they will have been cross-fertilised, you might create a wonderful new hybrid.

GENERAL

Order summer-flowering bulbs, such as gladioli, anemones and lilies.

Build up your strength. Next month is a busy one.

SOFT FRUIT AND FRUIT TREE PLANTING

The following table gives the approximate distance you should leave between each plant, tree or bush when planting:

	ft	m
Apples, cordon	2	60cm
Apples, bush	12	3.6
Apples, standard	25–30	7.6–9.1
Cherries, bush	15	4.5
Cherries, standard	30	9.1
Cob nuts	12	3.6
Currants	4–5	1.2–1.5
Gooseberries	4–5	1.2–1.5
Pears, cordon	2	60cm
Pears, bush	12	3.6
Pears, standard	25	7.6
Plums, bush	15	4.5
Plums, standard	25–30	7.6–9.1
Raspberries	2	60cm
Strawberries	1	30cm

APRIL

VEGETABLE PATCH

Watch the long-term weather forecast at the end of the *Farming* programme on BBC1 on Sundays at 12.55pm. If no frost is forecast, you should forgo your afternoon sleep and get some seeds sown. In theory the soil should be warming up.

Try to make sure that the seed bed is finely broken down. If you have used cloches to keep some areas of soil drier and warmer for early sowing, move some each weekend to create good conditions for sowing the next. All ordinary summer crops can be sown now, apart from tender runner and dwarf French beans. (See page 20 for seed germination times.) Get your onions in, and plant out any seedlings of the cabbage family that you sowed earlier. They should be about 4in. (10cm) high; if not, wait until they are. Onions and brassicas like lime and, of course, they need food.

When planting out, we are all tempted to try to win a bit extra by putting plants too close together. Try to visualise their size at maturity, and remember the hoe, that vital weedkiller: allow plenty of room for it, or you'll hoe up the plants.

It is tempting to use a soil pest killer against cabbage root fly, carrot fly, wireworms and other pests, but remember that it kills good bugs as well as bad ones. (See page 77 for some suggestions as to organic methods of pest control.)

LAWN

If your lawn is any size at all, it is probably worth spending money on a combined fertiliser and weedkiller, but wait until the grass is really growing before putting it on. *Don't* set the mower too low: ¾in. (2cm) is the minimum.

The best lawns are weed-free, frequently

fed and mown as necessary – sometimes as often as every other day. If that is too much work and too costly, try feeding less and you will need to mow less frequently. One of the editors gives his lawn a sprinkling of Growmore now and that's all for the rest of the year. He never sets the mower very low, and likes daisies, and the result is a good surface, tough enough to withstand children playing on it. He hardly ever collects the mown grass either, and brown patches, if not caused by his dog urinating on the lawn, are probably brought about by leather jackets eating the grass roots. If you think the latter is your problem, get a suitable insecticide from the garden centre.

Bare patches should be seeded. Sow a mixture of sand and seed, then scratch it in. If yours is a clay soil, wait until it is fairly dry before attempting this.

FLOWER BEDS & BORDERS

Hardy annuals (look at your seed packets) should be sown now. It is tempting to scatter the seeds, because regimented plants sown in

SEED GERMINATION TIME FOR VEGETABLES

Sown outside at the recommended sowing time, vegetables should be showing above ground within the following time scales. If not, you may have bad seed, may have sown it too deep, or have suffered some other disaster.

	Days		Days
Beans, broad	8–12	Leeks	21–24
Beans, French	10–14	Lettuces	10–15
Beans, runner	10–14	Marrows	6–10
Beetroot	18–24	Onions	21–25
Broccoli	7–12	Parsley	28–42
Brussels sprouts	7–12	Parsnips	21–28
Cabbages	7–12	Peas	7–12
Carrots	17–24	Radishes	6–10
Cauliflowers	7–12	Spinach	10–15
Celery	18–28	Swedes	7–12
Cucumber	5–15	Tomatoes	7–14
Endives	14–21	Turnips	7–12

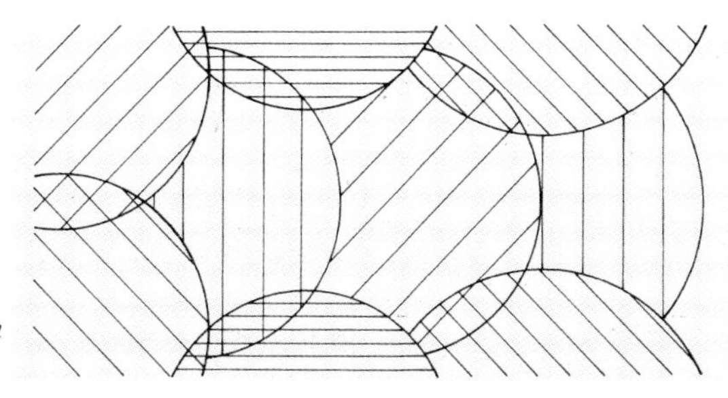

Mark out sowing pattern with a stick

lines don't look very pleasing. But if you do this, how can you distinguish the weed seedlings? Sown in short straight lines and half-circles, flower seedlings are easily recognised, and by the time they reach maturity their arrangement looks random.

Don't be in a hurry to sow half-hardy annuals.

Big clumps of herbaceous plants that flower late, like Michaelmas daisies, can be rejuvenated by splitting. As with rhubarb, discard the centre and re-plant the younger outside shoots.

Dead-head daffodils and tulips, but *don't* cut off the leaves, which are busy manufacturing food for next year's flowers. This is the time to move the bulbs if they are in the wrong place.

Roses need pruning now. It is a job that requires a bit of common sense. First, get rid of all branches that don't look completely healthy: the broken and diseased are no good; neither are spindly shoots, or those that grow across and crowd the plant. Then cut back what's left to buds on strong healthy branches. Whichever way the bud is pointing, that's the direction in which the new shoot will grow. So use your imagination and picture what the bush will look like when the bud you cut back to has produced 8 or 10in. (20 or 25cm) of shoot. In general, cut back to just above an outward-facing bud, so that you get an open structure that lets in light and air. If there is no bud to be seen, choose a leaf scar. Nine times out of ten there's a dormant bud hiding there.

If towards the end of the month you see bedding plants for sale, *don't* buy them. A few unscrupulous nurserymen grow two batches of plants for sale: the early ones that mostly succumb to frost and a later lot to replace them.

If you haven't yet spread and hoed in 2–3oz per square yard (50–75g per square metre) of Growmore, do it now.

HOUSEPLANTS, WINDOW BOXES, TUBS & TROUGHS

A high-potash feed (tomato fertiliser) will encourage flowering; give foliage plants a bit of ordinary fertiliser. All need water, and not too much. Touch the compost every day and, when it feels dry, soak the whole pot in the sink, then let it drain. Alternatively, leave the plant in its usual position, water generously from the top and empty out any water that remains in the saucer. Leave the plant until it feels dry again. Too much to drink every day will kill anything.

If you've sown seed in troughs and tubs you must ventilate. Cover with the glass or polythene only when frost is forecast. Conversely, the sun is getting stronger. Plants on south-facing windowsills will not like long periods of bright sun.

FRUIT TREES & BUSHES

There are some nasty insects about, and you can spray against them *before* the flowers open. Remember that bees are your best friends – they do sterling work in pollination – and if you kill them with spray, you won't have a crop.

WINDOWSILL, COLD FRAME & GREENHOUSE

Seedlings and cuttings on windowsills need to be rotated frequently to ensure that all the plants in the tray or pot get even light. Beware, however, of giving them too much sun.

The cold frame now comes into its own as the place to harden off young plants – that is, getting them used to colder nights and ready for the garden outside. Ventilation is vital, to minimise extremes of temperature and stop plants growing long and spindly. Use shading on sunny days – an old carrot bag.

If you haven't done so earlier, make sure you sow some courgette seeds in small pots on a windowsill. Courgettes are a wonderful vegetable and give excellent value.

TREES, SHRUBS & CLIMBERS

Winter-flowering heathers need a haircut or, more specifically, a dead-flower cut. Trim straggly bits, and then new growth will create a tidy shape. The same applies to early-flowering shrubs.

This is a good time to plant conifers and evergreens, but don't let them dry out. All those leaves lose water on warm windy days.

Try propagating by layering. Shrubs like rhododendrons and hydrangeas – or any with branches flexible enough to pin to the ground – are worth a try.

Climbers need feeding and a good mulch over the roots. Tie them in well to prevent wind damage.

If you've been planning to cover up some bare areas of wall or fence, go and buy the plant of your choice and put it in now. However, give careful consideration to the position: north-facing, west-facing or whatever. Read the plant label to make sure that it will thrive before parting with your money.

Any purely green shoots growing on a variegated shrub should be pruned out as they will not change colour later.

GENERAL

Trim hedges – unless birds have started nesting in them.

What you achieve by the end of the month dictates what the garden will look like throughout the summer.

WHY NOT GROW SOMETHING DIFFERENT?

BY ROY LANCASTER

Joe Lord was a dab hand at growing roses. Each summer his small privet-hedged garden in the suburbs of Southampton was a riot of colour as hybrid teas and floribundas combined to create a spectacle enjoyed by neighbours and passers-by alike. He even erected a rustic arch above his gate on to which he trained the rambler 'Albertine', because its light fragrance reminded him of his mother whose favourite this rose had been.

Roses apart, his garden supported the usual range of common and easily grown perennials among which cornflowers, catmint and London pride were prominent. As he was a widower and retired, his roses occupied much of his time, and when he was not outside tending to their needs he was inside studying catalogue descriptions and pictures of the latest introductions. Then, one day, something happened which changed his entire attitude to his garden and its contents and, in doing so, introduced him to a whole new world of plant experiences.

It was the annual flower show and Joe's roses, as usual, were among the prize winners. At one end of the big marquee was a small nursery stand, set up by a man and his wife specialising in the rare and unusual. Normally Joe would have passed by such displays without so much as a glance, but on this occasion his attention was caught by the name 'Chilean potato vine' on one of the paper labels. The very idea of a vine related to a potato amused him and he decided on a sudden impulse to buy the plant and have a go at growing it. He was told that it needed a warm sunny position and was best trained against a wall or fence. He knew exactly where he would plant it. A shed on the south side of his home had always been a bit of an eyesore, despite the roses he had established there, and he could not think of a warmer place.

It was the thought of growing something from sunny South America, however, that most appealed to him. Secretly he did not expect to succeed but it was, he decided, a chance worth taking, and if he failed it would not be the end of the world. As it was late in the summer when it was planted, the vine simply settled into its new position, throwing out a few strong green shoots without flowering. That winter Joe decided to protect the plant using a simple plastic screen supported on canes. He reasoned that it was the least he could do considering the severe conditions forecast. Despite cold winds and frosts which killed off the ends of the shoots, the potato vine survived, and once the days began to lengthen and the ground to warm up it commenced to grow with renewed vigour. Soon flower buds appeared at the shoot tips and on a sunny day in May the first flowers opened. They were, he had to admit, just like those of a potato, star-shaped and with a central 'beak' of stamens. Their colour, however, was a rich blue against which the yellow stamens were a striking contrast. All through that year the vine grew, pushing out bold clusters of its colourful flowers until the first frosts of autumn brought things to a halt.

All this happened a few years ago. Now Joe's potato vine covers the entire outhouse wall, hiding it through summer with wave after wave of exotic blooms. Such were the enquiries he received as to its name and origin that Joe did some checking among gardening books in the library to find the vine's real (botanical) name. He discovered it to be *Solanum crispum*, the second name referring to the crimpled leaf margins. From the colour and long-flowering nature of his plant he deduced that it belonged to a special selection named 'Glasnevin', which had originally been distributed by the National Botanic Garden, Glasnevin, Dublin, in the early years of the present century.

The satisfaction he got from his unexpected success pursuaded Joe to experiment with other unusual plants and it was not long before his roses were rubbing shoulders with more exotic neighbours with equally exotic names such as Californian lilac and orange ball tree. Not all his experiments have been successful, but does that deter him from further attempts? Not at all; it simply spurs him on to try again and if that fails to try something else.

Today his garden is far more colourful than it was and for longer too. To the riches of summer have been added those of spring and autumn and he even has plants which flower in the so-called dead of winter. An unexpected bonus has been the lessons he has had in botany, geography and history as a result of checking out details of each new plant. In effect, his garden has become a microcosm of the world's flora, with Chile, Mexico, Japan, China, Russia and New Zealand being just a few of the many countries represented.

I tell this story to illustrate how even the most dedicated specialist gardener can benefit from 'having a go' at something different. For those living, like Joe Lord, in the warmer areas of Britain, *Solanum crispum* 'Glasnevin' offers a relatively easy and rapid introduction to the world of exotic plants. So, too, does *Abutilon vitifolium*, also from Chile. This large shrub with bold, grey, downy, vine-shaped leaves is plastered from late spring through summer with large blooms like those of a single-flowered, pale lavender hollyhock. Even better is the variety 'Veronica Tennant' with larger flowers of mauve-blue, while 'Tennant's White' is a white version. Both these shrubs, given a warm sunny position in a well-drained soil, can reach at least 10–15ft (3–4.5m), and although a really hard winter can injure – if not destroy – them, they can be grown from half-ripened cuttings taken in summer and flower so early in life that the loss of the parent plant need not cause too much disappointment. They are more easily grown, by the way, from seed sown in March or April and, though the resultant seedlings will not be true to type, some lovely forms will nevertheless result.

For those who can provide sun and warmth but little in the way of elbow room there are a host of unusual plants available from specialist suppliers. One of these is *Erysimum* 'Bowle's Mauve', a sub-shrubby wallflower with narrow grey-green leaves and long spikes of mauve-purple flowers. This plant forms an evergreen mound up to 2ft (60cm) eventually, the flowers appearing continuously from spring into summer and occasionally in autumn as well. As with the abutilons, it is prudent to root a few cuttings of this plant each summer in case the parent plant is damaged or killed by severe winter conditions.

For something really unusual, though, how about a fuchsia-flowered gooseberry from California? Anyone handling the spiny stems of *Ribes speciosum* for the first time will need no convincing of its gooseberry connections, but their eyes will surely widen when, in late spring, the slender nodding crimson flowers appear in clusters along the undersides of the shoots. They really do have the appearance of fuchsias and never fail to cause comment from visitors. In warm areas of the country *Ribes speciosum* can be grown in a border or bed where it will make a wide-spreading bush up to 4ft (1.2m) high. In colder areas it needs the protection of a south- or west-facing wall where it is capable of reaching 5ft (1.5m) or more and as much across, especially if it is trained fanwise to wire supports. Old stems should be pruned away after flowering to accommodate the new ones which on an established plant are freely produced.

Now for an unusual perennial, a hardy plant which is suitable for almost any garden, even one as small as a pocket handkerchief. It is *Arisarum proboscideum*, whose second name – meaning proboscis – refers to the tail-like appendage to the flower, giving rise to its popular name, mouse-tail plant. It is a low-growing relative of the arum, producing in spring tufts and patches of glossy arrow-shaped leaves. The curious white and purple flowers appear in some quantity at the same time and would remain undetected if it were not for the slender, dusky, protruding tails. Lift up the leaves with your hand and you will see rows of flowers which look for all the world like tiny mice hiding their heads. Naturally it is a plant of immediate appeal to children and, given that it is easily obtained and easily grown, there is probably no better way of getting a child interested in the garden. It is grown from tubers which should be planted 6in. (15cm) deep, preferably in a moist soil in partial shade.

Another hardy herbaceous perennial worth growing is *Allium cernuum*, an ornamental onion from western North America. The idea of an ornamental onion may bring a smile to some people's faces, but there are simply scores of different kinds suitable for the garden, and in flowering qualities they are well able to hold their own with better-known perennials. The bulbs of *A. cernuum* should be planted in a group, when they will send up a sheaf of erect, rushy stems to 18in. (45cm), each stem carrying a nodding head of flowers which are enclosed in a pale green sheath like a bag. In mid-June the sheath splits and the small but rich amethyst-purple bell flowers emerge like an exploding rocket. It is easily grown in an ordinary soil in full sun and amply repays its keep.

So many people, not just Joe, find that the special responsibility and satisfaction of growing unusual plants add sparkle to their lives. Modern roses are beautiful in their own way but anyone can grow them and most people do. It is the curious and the exotic that really set the neighbours' tongues wagging and receive envious looks from other gardeners. A small garden a few doors away from me is dominated by an 18ft (5.5m) specimen of the Chilean fire tree, *Embothrium coccineum* var. *lanceolatum*, which in late May and June floods its branches with slender tubular flowers of a brilliant scarlet. It is a guaranteed show stopper and anyone in the western and southern counties of the British Isles who can offer this tree a sheltered site on an acid soil has a chance of making quite a name for themselves amongst the local gardening fraternity.

So, too, with the Australian snow gum, *Eucalyptus niphophila*, a relatively small, hardy tree of its kind whose star attraction is its beautiful marbled bark. This too requires a lime-free soil but it will grow quite happily in drier conditions than those enjoyed by the fire tree. For the ultimate in one-upmanship, however, it would be hard to beat the bristle-cone pines from the south-west United States of America, which qualify as the world's oldest living things. In the wild these pines grow on high mountain ridges in areas of low rainfall, conditions which, over the centuries, have resulted in individuals over 3,000 years old still alive and still growing. The bristle-cone pine normally available in Britain is *Pinus aristata*, a hardy, easily grown pine for almost any soil, attaining 20–30ft (6–9m) after thirty or forty years. Pines may not be every gardener's cup of tea, but to one with such a pedigree who can say no? Joe Lord is trying to find a place for it.

ALPINES

BY JOHN KELLY

One of the most fascinating things about alpines is the deep and abiding allure that they have for gardeners. Because of their size, the smallest of gardens can contain quite large collections of alpines, and because they consist of shrubs, herbaceous plants, bulbs and even small trees, the alpine gardener can enjoy a wide range of horticultural experiences while growing them.

It is a mistake to think that alpines are mostly spring-flowering. A great many of them are, but it is perfectly possible to have a fine display of flowers from the very early days of the year right into the late autumn, with a connecting thread of blooms through the winter. Grow alpines and you will find yourself compelled to leave your warm fire and go out into the garden to witness the rich blue flowers of *Iris reticulata* piercing the snow, or the little propeller-shaped blooms of *Cyclamen orbiculatum* defying the frost.

While the real specialists delight in growing extremely difficult plants from the world's highest mountains, the great majority of alpines are perfectly easy, and there are many different ways of accommodating them in gardens. The most usual is the rock garden; *not* a 'rockery' – the term should be banished from the language except, perhaps, to describe a place to grow rocks! How often one sees piles of lifeless, rubbly soil into which a few boulders have been thrust and upon which a few straggly, decrepit and decidedly elderly plants work out their pensions by producing a few tired flowers. The rockery is the skid row of gardening and the junkyard of horticulture.

What, then, is the difference between a rockery and a rock garden? The answer is that there is all the difference in the world. The distinction is between, on the one hand, a haphazard arrangement of any old soil and rocks, usually in the worst part of the garden and dictated by the position of one of those piles of builders' rubble or by where the ubiquitous 'fish pond' is to be put, and, on the other, a properly constructed home for alpine plants.

This will have been built with the needs of the plants in mind, as well as to fit the general design of the garden. In nature the soil that alpines grow in is very gritty because mountains are constantly eroding and the soils on them consist of larger and smaller fractions of rock mixed together with the decaying remains of plants and, usually, the droppings of the surprisingly large animal population. The soils are, in fact, quite rich, but are extremely well drained. They seldom dry out, either, except in places like Iran, as there is generally a constant supply of water from higher up where the snows are melting.

Rocks in nature, except where they have tumbled down in great unstable heaps where few plants grow, are arranged in strata, or layers. If you visit a mountainous area where outcrops of rock occur in grass, you will see that the rocks are in layers that have many vertical and horizontal fissures. These can easily be copied using good stone (sandstone or limestone are excellent; granite, or that frightful, glaringly white 'rockery' stone, are hopeless) so as to present a thoroughly natural appearance. In combination with a soil that is one half sharp grit and one half really good garden soil mixed with plenty of damp peat, such an arrangement is a true rock garden – not a rockery.

The soils should be rammed hard between the rocks and behind them so that each rock can be stood on without its moving. This prevents the making of dens by mice and pockets for slugs and ants' nests, and the soil rammed into the crevices between the rocks lets you grow plants there. Many alpines love to grow in vertical cracks between

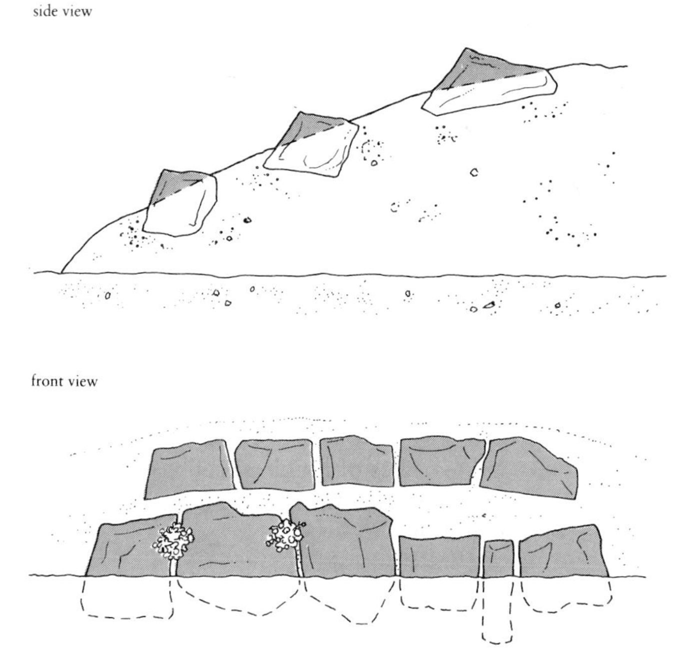

Arranging a natural-looking rock garden

stones; the trick is to put the plant next to the first stone and then jam the second stone against the roots of the plant, leaving the foliage free to spread over both of them. Any plant that dislikes having a wet neck in winter will be happy in such a situation, and some of the smaller tumbling plants will look perfect when growing from a crevice.

Weeds are the bane of the rock gardener's existence, although weeding is the best way of getting to know your plants. Weeds may be kept down a great deal by covering the soil surface with a generous layer of stone chippings – at least 1in. (2.5cm) deep – and this, too, will help to keep the vulnerable necks of the plants dry in winter. We should remember that alpines spend their winters under snow in nature and that snow is dry. Our winters are anything but dry and, although a great many alpines will put up with that, they will not do so if they are

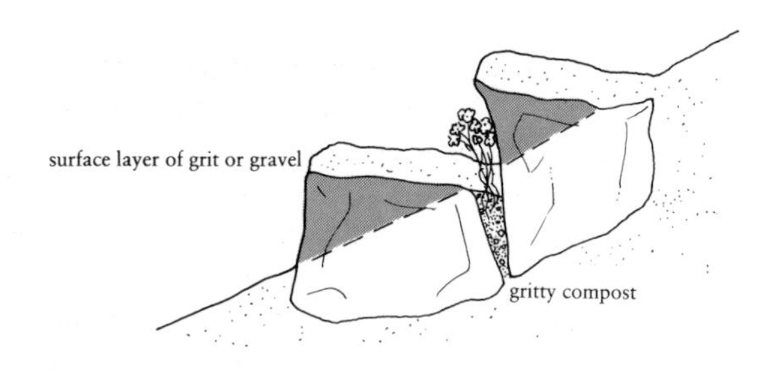

Planting an alpine

living in a claggy, soggy mess. A layer of chippings will also prevent rain splashing soil on to the foliage and making it look uncared for.

This layer of stone chippings is often incorrectly termed 'scree'. In fact a scree is a specific structure that is made for alpines whose dislike of winter wet is even greater than that of the easiest plants. Scree gardening is probably the best and most satisfying form of alpine gardening as the principles can be adapted to both raised beds and troughs – even the whole rock garden can be screes – and it is by no means difficult.

At the bottom of the scree is a layer of quite large stones – cobbles – and above these the stones gradually become smaller and smaller until the top 8in. (20cm) or so consists of a 50/50 grit and soil mixture. The whole thing can be of almost any depth from about 18in. (45cm) onwards, and this will depend on several factors. In clay soils, screes need to be deep, but an enormous amount of labour is needed to excavate a scree in clay, besides which one is liable to create a sump unless the water is led away by drainage pipes. The answer is to build it on top of the existing soil, either as a sloping component of the rock garden or confined within a raised bed. On light soils, too, the scree should be

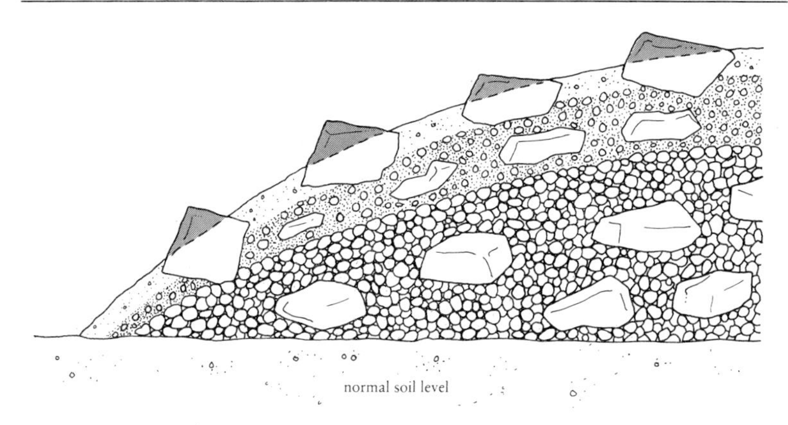

Making a scree garden

deep. The rich, gritty compost extends right down through the various grades of stones, and by making a deep scree you will have got over the essential dryness and hungriness of a very light soil.

In nature the roots of alpines go a very long way into the soil and between rocks and stones. Some plants, whose above-ground parts may be only 6in. (15cm) or so across, may have roots that are well over 6ft (2m) long. This is because they search far and wide for water and nutrients. If you allow them to follow this tendency to some extent in the garden, they will never suffer from drought or become uprooted by frost, and it is a fact that the better the root system, the better the plant. Most good rock gardens are based on the scree and, although they may take more work in their making, they give their owners years and years of happy gardening.

The raised bed is, in a way, the logical extension of the scree. In fact, most rock gardens made by experts are raised beds, although they may not look like it at first. This is because the surest way of obtaining good

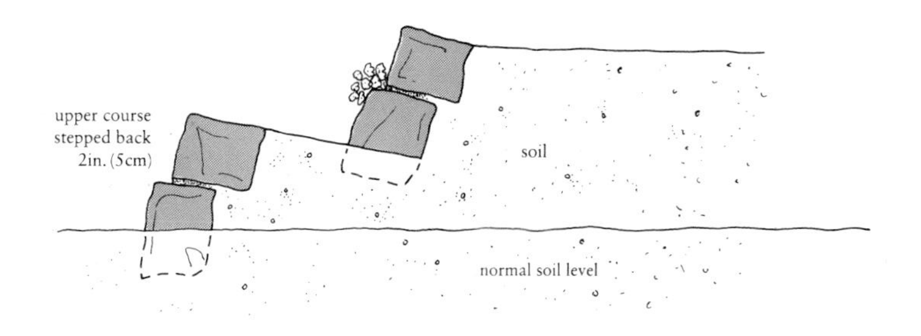

Making a raised bed

drainage is to build above ground level. Flat-topped raised beds, bounded by walls of rock a couple of feet high and constructed in tiers, can, if well-designed, look very natural indeed and in them a huge number of plants can be grown in quite a small space. They are very easy to work on, too, because you can sit on the walls as you weed or plant. It is a very good idea to furnish the beds with stepping-stones so that you do not tread on plants or on the places where bulbs are lying dormant, and so that you do not compact the soil with your weight.

Rock is expensive these days and the traditional rock garden is becoming beyond the reach of many people. The raised bed system, with the walls made from the much cheaper walling stone (bound by soil, not mortar, so that plants can be grown between the stones), is a good bet for the gardeners who want to grow alpines well. They will not only save their pockets, but will also be giving their plants the best chance of success.

Trough gardening is becoming increasingly popular now that it is more widely recognised that the containers can be made at home relatively easily. The old stone troughs are highly desirable, but hardly worth taking out a mortgage for, although you might be very lucky and pick one up for less than the dowry of a duchess.

If you are keen to save money by making your own 'stone' trough, you can follow these simple instructions. First, mix some soft concrete using 2½ parts sand, 1½ parts peat and 1 part fresh cement. Make a fairly sloppy mixture and pour the concrete into a large cardboard box to a depth of 1½in. (3.8cm). At this point, you reinforce your trough by pressing a piece of wire mesh into the bottom of the box, roughly to the middle of the layer of concrete. You will then need to press four 1½in. (3.8cm) wooden pegs through the concrete layer, one near each corner.

Now place a smaller cardboard box inside the larger one, leaving a

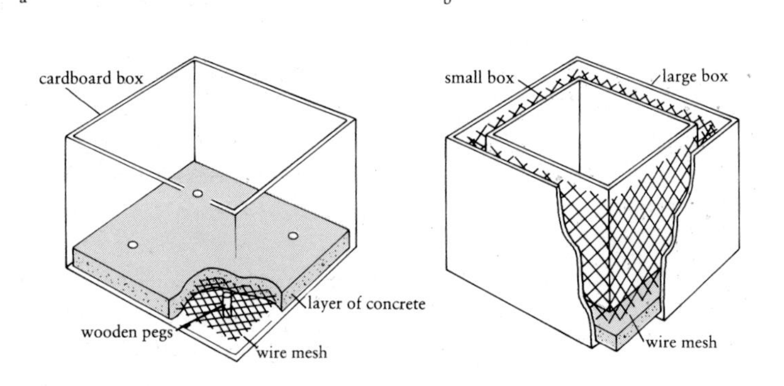

Making your own trough

gap of about 1½in. (3.8cm) all round and letting its base rest on the wooden pegs. For added strength, you must place some wire mesh round the smaller box so that it comes midway between the inner and outer walls. Then push in enough concrete to fill the gap between the two boxes, pressing it down well with a piece of wood. Fill the small box with bricks to give it support.

When you have filled the gap to the top, support the walls of the outer box with bricks and leave for twenty-four hours. Then tear off the outer box and roughly shape the walls of the trough with an old chisel and a wire brush. After an additional twenty-four hours (forty-eight hours in all), remove the inner box and roughly shape the inner walls. Leave for a week before removing the wooden pegs. Soak in milk to encourage moss to grow on the outside.

The trough is the complete controlled environment for alpines. Using the scree system, you control the soil and the drainage, and you can easily cover the plants in winter and so control the amount of moisture they receive. Troughs also look very nice and can be put anywhere in the garden. On the patio they not only look good, but they are also close to the house where their miniature beauty will be most appreciated. The tiniest city yard can become an alpine garden, even if every single plant is in a trough, and these containers look, to many eyes, rather more attractive than the pots and urns one more often sees in such places.

Alpines need very little care in comparison with most other types of plant. They do not need feeding, except when grown in troughs, where a little top-dressing of Growmore or some such fertiliser is essential from time to time. It is a good idea, however, when weeding to sprinkle a little fertiliser around each plant, but this should not be done often or at all heavily, otherwise the plants will grow soft and vulnerable to winter ailments. The scree system will provide them with just about all they need if it is made properly – a birthday treat, though, will cheer them up just like anyone else.

Alpines are remarkably pest-free, although they are martyrs to slugs. The best way of avoiding these creatures is to make sure that there are no holes and gaps where they can breed, but slug pellets should control them. Some dwarf conifers are highly susceptible to red spider mite. An infestation shows itself as a burn, followed by defoliation, and many gardeners mistakenly diagnose the trouble as wind-scorch. A spray with a systemic insecticide, applied twice in the year, in March and September, should eliminate the problem. Leaf miners can affect some plants and any trouble should disappear if a spray of HCH or triclorphon is applied towards the end of May and again later if necessary.

My own experience of growing many high alpines under glass – a road down which you will surely go one day, but that is another story – is that all insect pests can be controlled with one systemic insecticide, provided that a fresh supply is bought each year. This applies both outdoors and indoors.

Almost all alpines can be propagated either from soft cuttings in the spring or from seed. Cuttings are taken below a node from new growth as soon as it is big enough to handle and inserted in a half-and-half mixture of peat and sand in trays or pots. These are placed in a shaded cold frame which is kept shut until rooting starts, and the cuttings are sprayed with tepid water twice or three times a day. Soft cuttings root very quickly, and they should be potted on as soon as possible, otherwise they will soon grow long and lanky and become useless.

Seed should be sown in February or as soon as it is ripe, using a half-and-half mixture of sharp grit and a John Innes mixture without much fertiliser (Number 1 will do). The seeds are covered with ½in. (1cm) or so of coarse grit and left open to the elements in a frame which can be closed in the very worst weather. If cats are a menace, put some wire netting over the open frame. Some seed will not germinate for a year or two. Do not despair; look after it and its label and it will probably surprise you.

Very comprehensive seed lists are available to members of the Alpine Garden Society (see page 156 for the address). These organisations also produce very fine periodicals which are packed with information for all grades of gardener from beginner to expert, and there is likely to be a local group near you which holds meetings with speakers and the chance to exchange plants. Some of these host the regional shows at which, once the alpine 'bug' gets hold of you, you may one day find yourself exhibiting. The prize winners were beginners once themselves, after all.

TEN EASY ALPINES

Phlox subulata Several varieties, mostly pink or white. 'Temiskaming' is vivid magenta-red. Strongly growing, carpeters or tumblers. Spring.

Gentiana verna Usually seen as *Gentiana angulosa*, the vividly light blue spring gentian. Best grown in very gritty soil in drifts of at least ten plants.

Lithospermum diffusum 'Heavenly Blue' The most popular alpine of all time, but a lime hater. Easy in a peaty soil in full sun. Gentian-blue flowers for a long period in summer. Carpeting.

Geranium 'Ballerina' A summer-long succession of quite large flowers, lilac-pink with deep purple veining, over very neat foliage. 3in. (7.5cm) tall.

Narcissus 'Tête à Tête' Possibly the best dwarf daffodil for the open garden. Twin flowers of soft golden yellow on 5in. (12.5cm) stems. Early spring.

Saxifraga There are many alpine saxifrages. The cushion 'Kabschias' are wonderful in early spring – large flowers held tightly over neat buns. The 'Silvers' are looser, with panicles of white or pinkish flowers above rosettes of silvered leaves – they flower later.

Sempervivum The 'house leeks' are easy to grow anywhere in sun and will endure the poorest conditions. Their rosettes are the main attraction, although they flower in late spring and early summer.

Primula marginata Several varieties with flowers in blue, mauve and white. The leaves are prettily decorated with a creamy meal. Height: 4in. (10cm).

Cyclamen hederifolium The autumn-flowering cyclamen. Lovely in a shady place. Pink or white with marbled leaves.

Penstemon pinifolius A tiny shrub, 6in. (15cm) or so in height, with needle-like leaves and tubular flowers of glowing red. Flowers July/ August.

PLANT FOODS AND PLANT FEEDING

BY STEFAN BUCZACKI

On many occasions, when I have found myself involved in a discussion with gardeners on the subject of plant feeding and fertilisers, someone has posed the question of how wild plants manage without the intervention of you or me with our little bags of goodness. In essence they are asking how it can be that the soil of the woods and hedgerows is good enough for wild plants. Can we not, by logical extrapolation, diminish the use of chemicals in our gardens by similarly leaving our plants to fend for themselves?

The simple answer is yes, of course you can leave your plants to make what they will of the nutrients present in your garden soil. And depending on the amount of nutrient present, your beds and borders will still appear reasonably attractive for a limited period.

After a season or so, you will gradually notice a difference in the performance of the annuals and the herbaceous perennials, although the shrub border will probably change little for some time. But I would not put money on your chances of winning prizes with vegetables, or even with fruit.

The simple explanation will be apparent to anyone who has walked along the sea cliffs and seen a rather large, bluish-green, shaggy, loosely leaved plant among the cliff-top grasses and recognised it for what it is – wild cabbage. No one feeds and waters it, and if that is all you expect of the cabbages in your garden, you can happily do the same.

Quite simply, we have come to require rather more of our garden plants than the natural nutrients in the soil are able to provide, and especially is this true of vegetables, which we not only grow to a size and quality barely recognisable from their wild counterparts, we also expect the same plot of soil to provide the wherewithal for season after season. Is the message apparent? For a garden and garden plants worthy of the name, fertilisers are essential.

A visit to your local garden centre will certainly reveal the quite bewildering array of fertilisers that I found recently in mine. And your thoughts are, I am sure, those of the very worried-looking customer who said, 'Excuse me, but which do I need for my petunias?' To be perfectly honest, she could probably have used almost any of them, but there is a rhyme and reason to the world of fertilisers, which means that some blends are better for some plants than others.

So, let us start at the beginning. Fertilisers are mixtures of chemical compounds. When they are added to the soil and/or placed in water, they break down to their constituent parts and it is in these very much simpler forms that plants take up and make use of them.

Three chemical elements are more important to plants than others. They are often called the major nutrients, and I like to think of them as the main course of the plant's meal. These three are nitrogen, usually designated by its chemical symbol N; phosphorus, designated by the symbol P; and potassium, by K. (You will actually often read or hear of nitrates, phosphates and potash rather than nitrogen, phosphorus and potassium, but don't allow this to put you off.)

Almost all fertilisers contain N, P and K and on the packet you will see a percentage quoted for the amount present of each. They have different roles to play in plant growth although, surprisingly, there is still a great deal to be learned about their precise functions.

Nitrogen must be the most important of all, for it is a major constituent of protein, and of the protoplasm that makes up so much of a plant's bulk. For gardeners, nitrogen spells lush, leafy growth. Phosphorus too is involved in the chemical make-up of a wide range of important substances, including proteins, carbohydrates and fats. It is also especially important for seed germination and the ripening of fruit. Gardeners soon learn that it also promotes strong root development.

Potassium is the most mysterious of the three, but seems to be concerned with control of the water content of plant tissues, and to be involved with the process of photosynthesis, by which carbon dioxide and water from the air are converted in green tissues to carbohydrates. It also promotes the development of flowers and fruit.

So much for the main course. The dessert comprises a range of other chemical elements, of lesser importance in terms of quantity, but vital nonetheless for particular purposes. Calcium, for the development of strong cell walls, and magnesium as a constituent of the green photosynthesis pigment chlorophyll, are two of them.

Sulphur, manganese, boron, copper and molybdenum are also essential among these so-called trace elements, but in practice very few soils are actually deficient in any of them, and I am always a little sceptical about the claims made for fertilisers, largely on the grounds of the trace elements that they contain. I doubt very much if the trace element component of fertilisers plays a significant part in plant nutrition in most soils. And I am always puzzled when I am told that these substances improve the taste of fruits and vegetables.

For such an incredibly diverse spectrum of chemicals to influence the incredibly diverse spectrum of chemical processes that contribute to flavour, and always to do so in ways that we consider an improvement, stretches my credibility to the limit. There is, nonetheless, one of the minor elements to which I attach special significance, and that element is iron.

Plants need iron most of all in order to be able to manufacture chlorophyll, without which they function very inadequately. It is true that soils are rarely deficient in iron, but whenever a soil is markedly more limy than a particular plant prefers (and with the really acid-loving types such as rhododendrons and azaleas, this can occur at a very low lime level indeed), they are unable to take up the iron satisfactorily. So, in addition to fertilisers containing N, P and K, I believe that a fertiliser containing what is called 'available iron' is essential in many cases too.

Having shown our lady of the petunias which chemical elements she needs for her plants, there remains the problem of which specific packets to take from the shelf. Rather than selecting the so-called straight fertilisers like sulphate of potash, ammonium sulphate and so forth, which generally contain only one of the principal elements, buy those that offer some sort of blend.

Before giving my specific choices, however, I must mention two other important features of fertilisers. The first concerns in part the form in which they are made up, manufactured, or sold: fertilisers may be liquid or solid, fast-acting or slow-release. And, for the difference between a liquid and a solid fertiliser, I always draw an analogy with solid and soluble aspirin. If your headache is bad and you want the fastest possible cure, take an aspirin in soluble form, which will reach the parts where it is needed very quickly.

So it is with a liquid fertiliser. When plants are growing at a prodigious rate in the height of summer and need their meals in double-quick time, apply a liquid fertiliser and it will arrive post-haste, some of it actually being absorbed through the leaves by what is called foliar feeding.

There are differences in speed of availability among solid fertilisers too. Some, like dried blood or, to a degree, Growmore, break down very rapidly in the soil to liberate their active chemical principles. These are useful, therefore, right at the start of the growing season to give plants an early boost, while remaining in the soil long enough to have some slightly persisting action. Bonemeal, on the other hand, breaks down very slowly and releases its important phosphate component at a measured pace for the roots of long-lived perennials to absorb over a period of weeks or months.

There is a second factor to consider, and one that seems to have assumed increasing importance in recent years: the choice between an organic and an artificial fertiliser. Unfortunately, one of the difficulties here is that of definition. For while an artificial fertiliser is quite clearly one manufactured, like ammonium sulphate, in a chemical factory, an organic fertiliser ought to be obtained from some once-living organism – bonemeal or hoof and horn, for instance. Where, then, do the likes of rock potash lie, dug as they are from the ground? The organic gardener, in fact, regards these as organic materials.

Although there are undoubted arguments against the excessive use of any fertiliser, and although high usage of some artificial nitrogen fertilisers in particular can lead to contamination of the environment, there is in my opinion no intrinsic reason why a particular fertiliser should be better or worse for plants merely because it is or it isn't organic. (See, however, Geoff Hamilton's views on this subject in 'A Basic Guide to Organic Gardening', page 70.) Nonetheless, some organic fertilisers, like bonemeal and hoof and horn, are particularly useful, not because they are organic, but because they are slow-release in action. It really is a case of horses for courses.

Thus, having suggested guidelines for how you make your choice, I will offer what I consider a useful short list of fertilisers which will take care of most gardening needs.

First must come a balanced, general-purpose fertiliser. By a balanced fertiliser, I mean one in which the amount of nitrogen (remember, the most important element of all) is at the most generally useful level, and where the amounts of phosphorus and potassium likely to be needed have been adjusted accordingly.

Growmore is the best artificial fertiliser of this type; blood, fish and bone the best organic blend, although the proportions of N, P and K are somewhat different.

HOW MUCH LIME?

Your soil's lime requirements per square yard/metre – hydrated or garden lime:

Acidity (pH)	Soil Type Sandy		Loam		Clay		Peaty	
oz	oz	g	oz	g	oz	g	oz	g
6.5	0	0	0	0	0	0	0	0
6.0	2½	65	2½	65	5½	160	0	0
5.5	4	125	5½	160	8	250	8	250
5.0	5½	160	8	250	10	300	16	500
4.5	8	250	10	300	14	400	24	750
4.0	8	250	14	400	16	500	32	1000

Second, you will need a fast-acting liquid fertiliser, high in potash, for feeding flowering and fruiting plants during the growing season. Most of the popular brand leaders among liquid fertilisers, and also the liquid tomato fertilisers, are of this type.

Third, you should have two lawn fertilisers: a blend high in nitrogen for spring and summer use, and also one lower in nitrogen for autumn use. (Too much nitrogen late in the season will give rise to soft lush foliage, prone to damage and disease in the winter.)

Next, do have a stock of bonemeal which will be invaluable whenever you are planting herbaceous perennials, trees and shrubs, and also other long-lived plants such as bulbs and corms.

Finally, remember my comments about iron and buy a fertiliser called sequestrene. This contains iron in a form that plants are able to absorb, even on very limy soils, and it should be applied routinely to all acid-loving species at the start of the season and also used as a tonic for any plant showing unnatural yellowing of the foliage.

Two final suggestions: first, see page 10 for how to make a simple and accurate volume measure for fertiliser. And second, note the following list, which indicates the amount of Growmore to use for the most commonly grown vegetable crops:

	Amount of Growmore Recommended	
Crop	**oz/sq.yd**	**g/sq.m**
Pea	0	0
Carrot	1	25
Radish	1	25
Broad bean	3	75
Parsnip	3	75
Lettuce	4	125
Onion	4	125
Broccoli	5	150
Dwarf bean	5	150
Leek	6	175
Potato	7	200
Beetroot	7	200
Spinach	7	200
Cauliflower	7	200
Brussels sprout	10	300
Cabbage	10	300

SUMMER

MAY
JUNE
JULY

CUTTINGS
John Kelly

THE WORRY OF WEEDS
Clay Jones

A BASIC GUIDE TO
ORGANIC GARDENING
Geoff Hamilton

MAY

VEGETABLE PATCH

If the windowsills are cluttered and the cold frame bulges with leeks, Brussels sprouts, cauliflowers and cabbage, watch the weather forecast, cross your fingers and plant them out.

Any spare bits of ground can be sown with just about anything you choose. You'll get a crop sooner or later. And later is important: do you want winter cabbage and broccoli?

Get out the hoe and keep those weeds down. If they grow up to seed, you'll have them in abundance for years. Dine like a lord on asparagus. If you haven't got any, why not find out about planting some? It takes a year or two to establish.

LAWN

Mow the lawn when necessary. Often is easier and creates a better, thicker turf. This is because grasses tiller – that is, small shoots grow from the base of the bigger ones. If there is enough light, they get stronger and grow on. If not, they are smothered, and wither and die. On a small lawn, why not dig up the weeds with a kitchen fork? Alternatively, put a spot of salt or herbicide on each one.

FLOWER BEDS & BORDERS

Plant out dahlia tubers, and remember that the shoots, when they appear, are like asparagus to slugs, as are the shoots from herbaceous perennials. Kill the slugs (see pages 11 and 78), or suffer the consequences: good plants lost and big gaps in the border.

There are so many good perennial flowering plants – the perfect answer for the proud but lazy gardener. Most can be sown now, preferably in rows in a small nursery bed. In a square yard you can grow enough to provide joy to you and your friends for years. Transplant them to their final positions in September. Sow biennials too. Wallflowers and sweet

Williams are musts, but what about Canterbury bells, honesty, columbines and, best of all, foxgloves?

Roses need spraying once a fortnight. Combined insect and disease control in one go is easy now, sold in a packet in every garden centre.

It is perhaps late, but by now safe, to plant summer-flowering bulbs. Gladioli and crocosmia give colour and height to a border.

It is very important when putting in bedding plants to be sure that their roots are wet *before* going into the ground and that, once in, they are watered again to wash the soil particles in close to the roots. Logically, the same applies to young vegetable transplants.

HOUSEPLANTS, WINDOW BOXES, TUBS & TROUGHS

Keep an eagle eye on plants so that you spot insects like whitefly and red spider mite when they first appear, not after they've multiplied and caused real damage. *Do not spray* in the house unless you have no alternative, in which case use a dustbin liner as a sort of tent around the plant. It is a bit of a juggling act, but stops spray drifting on to the curtains and up your nose.

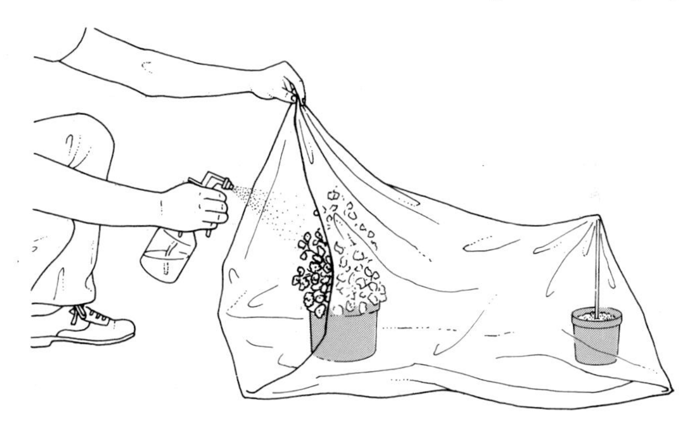

Using a dustbin liner for indoor spraying

The inclination of most plants is to grow tall and thin, because a lot of energy goes to the top growing point on the main stem. Snip that off and a plant will grow its side shoots much more vigorously and become a more compact bushy specimen. To train it to the shape you want, remove some of the side shoots as well.

Take care not to overwater houseplants, and give them a liquid feed once a fortnight. (If that seems a chore, there are slow-release pellets and sticks of fertiliser that last for two or three months.)

FRUIT TREES & BUSHES

Remember that most fruit is 80 to 90% water, hence trees and bushes need moisture in dry periods just as much as vegetables and flowers. If you haven't mulched, do so now (see page 45 for more information), and if you haven't got enough compost to mulch, water the roots whenever you water anything else. Fruit growing up a wall gets particularly thirsty, except apricots.

The codling moth is an especially unpleasant pest. You don't see its maggoty offspring until you bite into the apple. If you don't like spraying, or if it is too much trouble, try a pheromone trap (see page 79).

If spraying against any other insect pests – and there are plenty about – *don't* do it when the trees or bushes are in full flower or you will kill the bees and other 'friendly' insects.

WINDOWSILL, COLD FRAME & GREENHOUSE

In theory the windowsill should be clear of young plants; they should by now have been moved to the cold frame to be hardened off ready to go out into the garden.

Extremes of temperature are a problem. There are sunny days when frames and houses get very hot, followed by cold nights. Shade and ventilation are the watch words.

Moulds, mildews and fungi flourish in warm damp conditions, and a recommended dose of Benlate in the watering can is a useful preventive every now and again. Spraying against pests before they appear in numbers is well worthwhile. Feed everything: you cannot

WHAT IS A MULCH?

A mulch is a layer of well-rotted compost, grass clippings, manure, chipped bark or similar material that is applied to the surface of the soil. The reason for mulching is threefold:

■ To provide a protective layer from cold or drying out – particularly important for tender herbaceous plants.
■ To provide nutrients.
■ To keep weeds down.

A mulch should be loose-structured and at least 2in. (5cm) thick. Newly planted roses, trees and shrubs need a mulch, but be sure to water well *before* putting it on.

expect really good growth without providing the nutrients.

TREES, SHRUBS & CLIMBERS

From a plant's point of view, the sole object of producing a flower is to attract an insect to fertilise its female part, which will then develop into a seed. Naturally the plant puts a lot of energy into seed development and our interests are usually to divert that energy into new and stronger growth. Therefore removing young seed heads straight after flowering is an important job.

Get to know your shrubs. Rhododendrons and azaleas have buds right next to the old flowers, so dead-heading (not essential, but well worthwhile) must be done by hand; others need pruning back quite severely – the information on page 51 will guide you. Borrow a book from the library to make sure that you get the technique right.

With climbers, like clematis, it is very important to know exactly what you are doing when it comes to pruning. If in doubt, *don't*. If the plants are straggly but vigorous, you can tidy them up by restrained pruning and tying them up neatly.

GENERAL

Weeds are the number one enemy. Get at them when they are small!

JUNE

VEGETABLE PATCH

It is still not too late to sow a vast number of vegetables. Any transplants or young bought-in plants need to be watered in well to make sure that the roots are in good contact with soil particles. They need a lot of water if the weather is at all dry until they are very well established.

The cabbage root fly causes havoc and disappointment in many a garden because its grubs eat away the roots just as the plants are getting away strongly. A small collar made from an offcut of rubber-backed carpet or underlay, tucked neatly round the stem of any plant in the brassica family at the time it's put out, minimises the success of this pest (see page 78).

If you have not been growing calabrese from seed, go out and buy some young plants. They are a good investment, because you only pick as much as you need and they go on yielding well for weeks and weeks. If they produce more than you want, remember that it is a vegetable which freezes very well.

Keep hoeing the weeds, except amongst the

YIELD: VEGETABLES

Approximate yield you can expect per square yard (metre) of vegetables:

	lb	kg		lb	kg
Beans, broad	2	1	Cauliflowers	3	1.5
Beans, French	1½	750g	Leeks	5	2.25
Beans, runner	5	2.25	Lettuces	10–13 heads	
Beetroot	5½	2.5	Onions	5½	2.5
Broccoli	3¾	1.7	Parsnips	5	2.25
Brussels sprouts	2	1	Peas	1½	750g
Cabbages, spring	4	2	Potatoes, maincrop	5	2.25
Cabbages, autumn	4	2	Shallots	8	3.6
Cabbages, winter	7	3.1	Spinach	3¾	1.7
Carrots, early	3¾	1.7	Swedes	6	2.75
Carrots, maincrop	6½	2.9	Turnips	6	2.75

onions. They don't like having their roots disturbed, so hand weeding is safer, and they do like regular feeding. So does everything else in the vegetable patch.

LAWN

Mow on sunny dry evenings, then sit in a deckchair with a glass in your hand and admire your work. Obviously lawns are very thickly planted, so in dry periods the need for water is as great as or greater than that in any other part of the garden.

FLOWER BEDS & BORDERS

When buying bedding plants, go for healthy specimens. If they look a bit yellow and tired, don't buy them. Good plants will have had the main growing tip pinched out to encourage the side shoots to grow. Snip off a few more growing tips before planting to get really bushy plants with lots of flowers, and make sure they get a good soaking every day for the first week or two that they're in the soil.

Weeds grow faster and pests proliferate in June. Even the laziest gardener cannot avoid taking up the hoe and the spray to do battle. (See page 62 for information on controlling specific pests.)

Roses should start to flower now. When

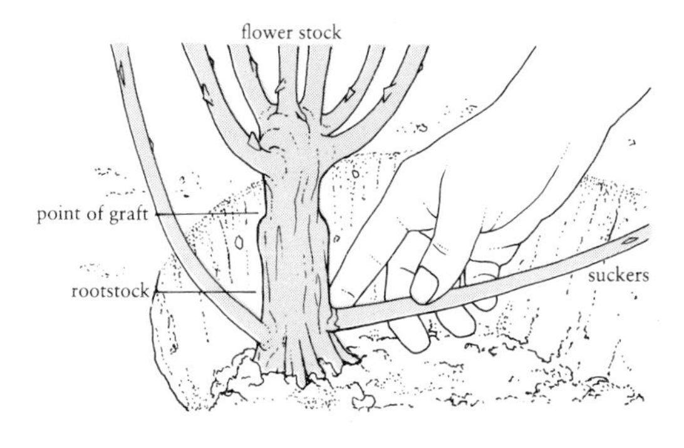

Removing suckers from roses

each flower is over, remove it. Many roses are grown on rootstocks; that means that the stem that produces the flowers is quite different from the rose root on which it grows. They've been grafted together to get more vigour and more flowers from the variety above the ground. So the rootstock below, the energetic bit, often sends up suckers, which are stems of its own. If allowed to grow, they will eventually take over from the rose you bought. So remove suckers on sight, and don't just cut them off at ground level, for that way they will multiply. Burrow down the sucker stem to the point at which it emerges from the main root, and pull it off there.

With a bit of wire and ingenuity you can devise supports for tall herbaceous plants that are far tidier than canes and lengths of string.

HOUSEPLANTS, WINDOW BOXES, TUBS & TROUGHS

Geraniums and pelargoniums are wonderful, indoors and outdoors; and, mixed with bedding plants of all sorts in window boxes and hanging baskets, they cheer up the aspect of any house. Remember, however, that pelargoniums are very frost-tender and that any plants grown close together in small boxes, tubs, troughs or baskets need a lot of looking after. They need watering *every day*, even when it rains. They need feeding at least once a week, and dead-heading fading flowers is a

HOW TO KEEP A GREENHOUSE OR FRAME HUMID

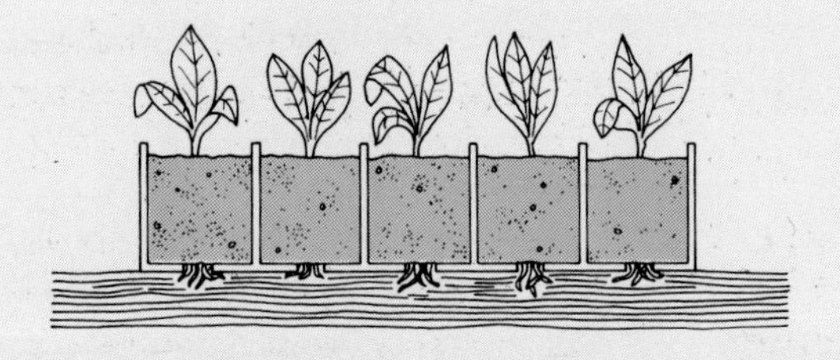

Spread a thick layer of newspaper on the greenhouse or cold frame shelves or floor. Soak thoroughly before putting your trays of seedlings on top. When watering, be sure to give the newspaper a dose so that it never dries out. It provides humidity round the plants, and roots will spread into the paper. This is particularly successful with propapacks.

must. In fact, they demand the same attention as the cat.

Foliage plants indoors will appreciate a spring clean. Wash the leaves with tepid water, or better still put them outside for an hour or two on a warm drizzly day. *Do not* leave them out in strong direct sunshine or during a cold night.

Try your hand at stem and leaf cuttings. Small plants in tiny pots probably need to go into one size larger. When you can see roots coming through the hole in the bottom, it's time to re-pot.

FRUIT TREES & BUSHES

Thinning fruit clusters

Keen growers thin the small fruits to make sure that the branches do not have to bear too heavy a load. Others wait for the 'June drop', when nature does the job for them. Often nature overdoes it, but there is nothing you can do to stop it.

However, it is logical that if you want large individual fruits of any kind, you have to consider the tree or bush on which they grow, and not ask it to produce too many. So thin if you wish. It is essential to summer-prune fruit trained as cordons and espaliers. If you have done the training yourself, you will understand what it is all about. If you've inherited them, get a good book and study it carefully before wielding the secateurs.

The rest of us, with no cordons or espaliers, should forget about summer pruning, as it is easy to do more harm than good.

WINDOWSILL, COLD FRAME & GREENHOUSE

If you haven't thought of it before, why not go down to the garden centre and buy three melon plants and a grow bag? You can get a crop in a cold frame as well as in a greenhouse.

With grow bags, although it seems to be seldom recommended, we think it is a good idea to cut 2in. (5cm) slits every foot (30cm) or so on either side at ground level. This

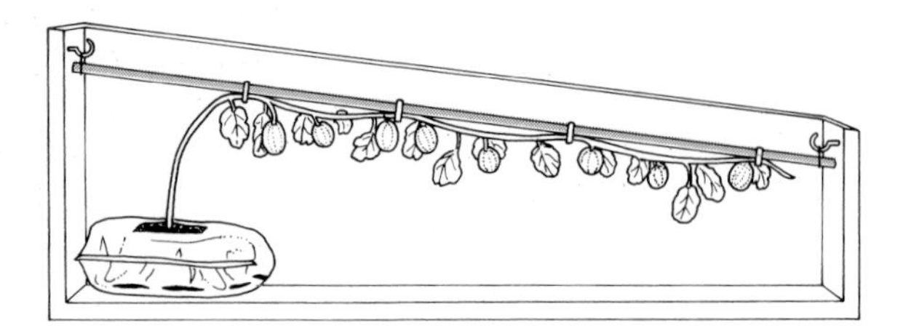

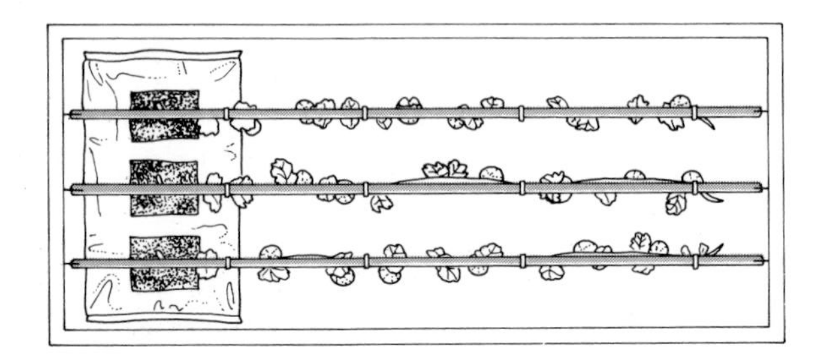

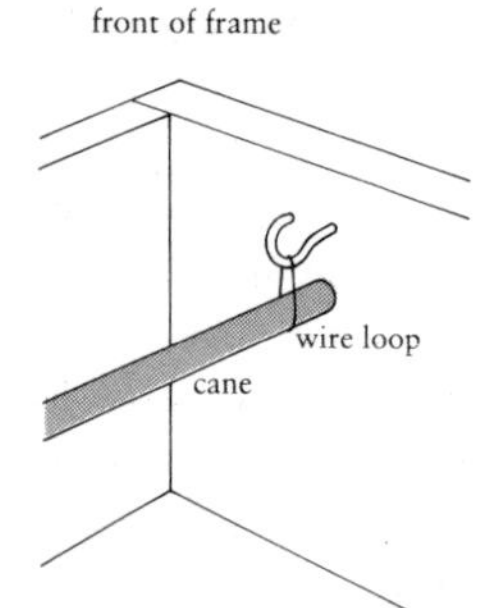

Growing melons in a cold frame

means that if you do overwater, there is some drainage and your tomatoes, or whatever, are not left trying to survive in a plastic pool of soggy peat. You quickly learn how much water and food is needed by the plants. If it weeps out at the bottom, you're giving too much.

On hot sunny days the humidity in the greenhouse and cold frame drops dramatically, and plants need humidity. So don't just water the pots and grow bags, water the floor as well, whether it is soil or concrete (and see page 48 for further tips). Making sure that plants have ventilation and spraying water around the place is a pleasant task each morning before setting off for the daily toil.

TREES, SHRUBS & CLIMBERS

Continue dead-heading rhododendrons and azaleas (see page 45) and prune back other shrubs after they've flowered to tidy them up.

The most fun this month is undoubtedly in trying to root cuttings (see page 57). Your favourite shrubs, either in your own garden or someone else's, will have dozens of vigorous young shoots.

Young trees and shrubs, particularly evergreens, need plenty of water. Why do we tend to forget them while looking after vegetables and flowers diligently? Newly planted evergreens benefit from a frequent shower over the leaves. If God doesn't provide it, you can.

There are a dozen and more good climbers and wall plants, apart from the perennial ones. In many areas of the country some perennials are better grown annually. One superb example is the Chilean glory vine, *Eccremocarpus scaber*. If your garden centre doesn't supply young plants, suggest to them that they should.

Climbers can be grown in tubs as well as directly in the ground, and we all have enormous barren wastes on the walls of our houses that could become pictures. However, they grow fast and need tying in to good supports. Brass hooks are best.

GENERAL

Have you planted out young winter veg plants? If you haven't grown them, go and buy them.

Given a bit of decent weather, you cannot avoid weeding and watering. Try very hard to enjoy your gardening. You've got over the worst bit apart from the lawn!

PRUNING ORNAMENTAL SHRUBS

Ornamental shrubs fall into three main groups:

- Those that produce flowers on the previous season's growth (for example, forsythia, philadelphus and ceanothus). Prune immediately after flowering by taking out most of the shoots that have born flowers to a point above where replacement buds are growing.
- Those that produced flowers on this season's growth (for example, *Buddleia davidii*, *Hydrangea paniculata*, artemisia). Cut hard back on the previous season's growth and leave new growth.
- Those that require very little pruning (for example, rhododendron, camellia, euonymus, elaeagnus, acers, daphne, pernettya, photinia, viburnum). Simply thin occasionally and remove crossing and diseased branches. You can shape the shrub or tree if it is aesthetically displeasing.

JULY

VEGETABLE PATCH

The exquisite taste of newly dug potatoes, boiled until just cooked with a large sprig of mint, should be yours at the prod of a fork. If you are greedy and want maximum yield with every potato the size of a fist, water the plants generously, even when it rains.

All the vegetable plants will almost certainly need water, and some fertiliser.

Be optimistic, and on the area vacated by potatoes sow beetroot, French beans, carrots, salads – whatever takes your fancy. Start them under a cloche. Think ahead to winter, and sow spring cabbage too.

LAWN

The damn thing still needs cutting, and if there's a dry spell, set the blades higher. If there are water restrictions, the lawn is the last consideration, but if there are none, soak it generously. This rule applies to watering any plant: too little can do more harm than good, for the roots then stay on the surface instead of going down deep into the soil.

FLOWER BEDS & BORDERS

All plants need water and food to produce to their maximum. Be generous with both and they'll flower profusely. Removing fading blooms from plants like nemesia and violas is a bit tiresome, but it pays dividends in further flowers; with roses it really is important.

When cutting off dead rose flowers, have a good look at the plant. Despite the impeccable pruning that you did at the beginning of the year, your rose bush will inevitably have shown its independence and grown branches across and up the middle. Hopefully these will produce wonderful flowers, and as soon as they start to fade, you should remove the whole branch. Don't throw it away, however: 1ft (30cm) of stem, with one set of leaves left near the top, pushed 6in. (15cm) into the soil,

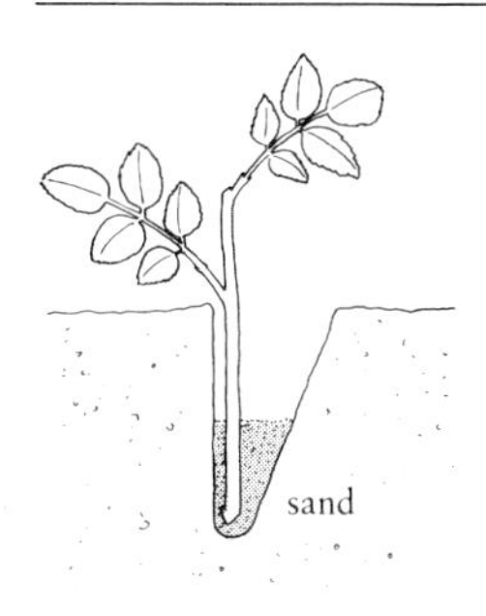

Rooting a rose cutting

will more often than not take root.

There is no more satisfying gift than the instant offer of a rooted cutting to someone who admires one of your roses, though there is a snag. Your rose is probably grown on a rootstock to give it extra vigour. So your gift may turn out to be a bit weedy. On second thoughts you may decide to try it for a year or two yourself, before damaging a lifelong friendship. But getting something for nothing is fun. Give it a try.

Your biennials – wallflowers and so on – will need thinning to produce strong plants. If you've forgotten to sow them, do it now. Have a good look round the garden centre for autumn-flowering bulbs. Keep the hoe shiny and knock out those weeds.

HOUSEPLANTS, WINDOW BOXES, TUBS & TROUGHS

Water, feed, and remove dead flowers. In theory this is high summer, so the humidity is low. Houseplants generally like a moist atmosphere, so keep a small sprayer filled with water near them. (You can buy quite decorative-looking ones.) Give them a squirt as you pass by; pure water won't harm the curtains or the furniture. Take cuttings.

FRUIT TREES & BUSHES

Blackcurrants taste better if they're left on the bush for a week or two after they've turned black: they are sweeter. After picking, prune out a third of the old wood – next year's fruit grows on the new wood. Or you could prune first, then pick the fruit off the cut stems in comfort. You are aiming for a nice open bush, as shown in the illustration.

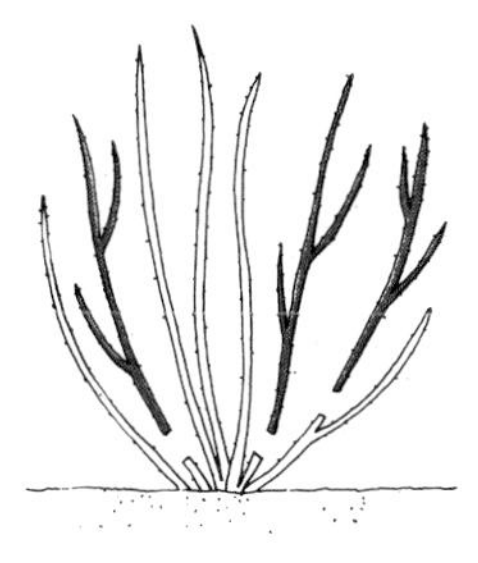

Pruning a blackcurrant bush

The birds are just as keen on fruit as you are. Netting is an expensive answer, or train the cat to walk around every half-hour.

Watering is very important, especially for trees and bushes close to walls. Remember that fruit has a high water content.

WINDOWSILL, COLD FRAME & GREENHOUSE

Even if recent experience suggests the contrary, you should expect a lot of sunshine, so frames and greenhouses need shading. Ideally they should have been done a month or more ago. You can now buy a preparation that you spread on, which leaves a white film over glass and polythene and is easy to wash off at the end of the season. Ventilation is vital, and you should continue spraying water about to keep up the humidity.

If you like taking cuttings, a small cold frame with 4 or 5in. (10 or 12.5cm) of peat and grit on the bottom is an ideal medium to stick in a young shoot of anything and everything that you want more of. Cover it with a bit of green netting and label your cuttings: only elephants never forget.

TREES, SHRUBS & CLIMBERS

Like everything else, water and food are fundamental needs. Prune back shrubs after flowering, and take cuttings. Climbers will be growing vigorously, and the new growth is tender and easily damaged in the wind. Tie in these shoots firmly, and do the same with new growth from shrubs grown against the wall. Shape them by pruning unwanted new growth. The plant then puts its energy into the areas you want it to.

GENERAL

This is the boasting season. Amongst your vegetables or flowers, or both, you are bound to have one or two outstanding successes. You can be sure that this is nature's doing and not yours, so don't bore the pants off your friends and neighbours!

A DIFFERENT SWEET PEA FRAME

If you think a wigwam of canes is ugly, and you haven't got a pergola, try to get hold of a young unwanted tree, or some 7ft (2m) branches. Don't trim; just plant firmly upside down, and grow your sweet peas up them. They get into a tangle at the top, but it looks quite effective.

CUTTINGS

BY JOHN KELLY

We inhabit a world in which we are surrounded by evidence of the will to live. Nature provides us with innumerable examples of survival as the prime motive of all life, with reproduction (which is survival in another form) running a close second. Why, then, is it that as soon as a gardener gets his hands on a plant he becomes convinced of its desire to curl up and die at the first opportunity?

Heaven knows. But it is so. And it is also true that the gardener's belief in the death wish in plants leads him or her to be convinced that only a mixture of mumbo-jumbo and magic will induce plants to reproduce themselves by means other than seed. That a piece of a plant should want to grow roots and survive seems to gardeners extraordinary, although they may be plagued to death by couch grass and docks, every broken bit of which has the reproductive proclivity of a rabbit.

That some cuttings are difficult is true. There are even a few that are very difficult indeed. I would not expect to be able to strike a cutting of a eucalyptus or of *Camellia reticulata*, and I would anticipate a high failure rate with pines, but the vast majority of plants can be rooted by the average gardener. The major requirement is not a matter of spells, or of the mythical green fingers; it is thought.

A great deal of good gardening is all about thinking straight, and the thinking gardener will have spotted that leaves give off water and that roots take it up. He or she will then have worked out that if the water lost by the leaves of a plant exceeds that taken up by the roots, the plant will wilt first and then die. A cutting with leaves on has no roots, but is getting rid of water very quickly, so the first essential is to put a stop to the process so that the cutting can adjust itself by growing some roots just as soon as possible.

At this stage the thinking gardener will point out that some cuttings – the hard-wooded ones, taken after leaf-fall – have no leaves, and he or she will straight away have found the major classification of cuttings into two groups: leafy and non-leafy cuttings.

LEAFY CUTTINGS

Preventing the loss of water from leafy cuttings is pretty simple. An environment is created for them from which water cannot escape, or, at the very least, escapes only very slowly. This is done by covering them with glass or polythene so that the pots or trays in which they are set

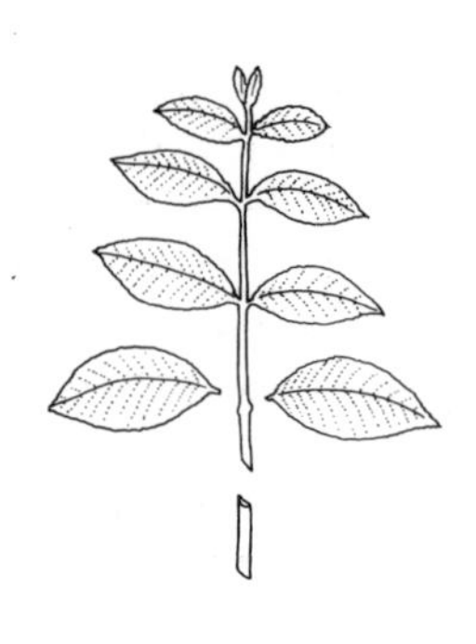

Preparing a leafy cutting for rooting

Rooting several cuttings in a pot

are completely enclosed. They will then themselves contribute to creating a highly humid atmosphere, to which will be added the water that evaporates from the compost. What little water escapes can be replaced if the cuttings are given a light spray of tepid water occasionally.

A cold frame can be used for large numbers of cuttings, or a few can be inserted in a pot which is then enclosed in a polythene bag, held away from the cuttings by wire hoops. Where failures occur tends to be where the air space is too great for the amount of water that is available to fill it. Too large a frame can never become saturated with water vapour, and it should be remembered that the cuttings themselves occupy space. It is always recognised that one cutting of a plant will often fail to root, while several will succeed. This is nothing to do with Murphy's Law; it is simply that, in the case of the single cutting, there is too much space and not enough water vapour.

Friends should, for this reason, always be offered as many cuttings as you can afford – never just one. It is worth noting, too, that a friend who is a good propagator will not turn his nose up at some cuttings at any time of the year. There is, it is true, a 'best' time of year for most cuttings, but it is surprising what will root when you would least expect it. The will to survive is extremely strong and plants will always try to root and may well succeed at completely the 'wrong' time of year. I once obtained a 100% strike with cuttings of *Magnolia grandiflora* (an evergreen) after the tree had collapsed under the weight of snow – in January!

Cuttings have within them food and hormones. The food reserves will keep them going until the new roots can supply more, and will also be topped up by the action of light on the leaves. They need to be shaded against direct sunlight, but too much shade will prevent their rooting because the leaves will cease to act and the hormones will not work either.

The hormones – the substances that govern growth – are concentrated in those parts of the stems where the leaves arise (the nodes). It is from these nodes that new roots will develop and it is at a point just below a node that the cutting is severed from its parent.

The lowest pair of leaves on the cutting are now removed, but, depending on the length of the cutting, it may be a good idea to take away more leaves from higher up, because they will only serve to act as losers of water. Usually, just one or two pairs of leaves are left on the cutting. In the case of alternately leaved plants, the node gives rise to one leaf only, but three or four leaves will still be left.

In general, cuttings will be inserted for about the lowest third of their length into the compost. Gardeners tend to have their own recipes for this, but I have found that a half-and-half by volume mixture of peat and sharp sand is as good as or better than anything else, although the sand should be lime-free if plants like camellias, rhododendrons, azaleas or summer heathers are being propagated. Some of my colleagues like to use peat and vermiculite and tend to recommend it. The fact that their results are as good as mine bears them out and reinforces the view that dogmatism in gardening is folly; the 'best' method is the one that works for you.

Similarly, I would not disagree too violently with those who use hormone rooting powders on all the cuttings that they take. I prefer, however, to reserve their use for cuttings that I know to be less than easy – camellias, deciduous azaleas and *Lithospermum* 'Heavenly Blue', for instance – because I have found by experiment that with a very large range of cuttings their use is unnecessary and may in some cases actually retard rooting.

The powders that are sold at garden centres are correctly formulated

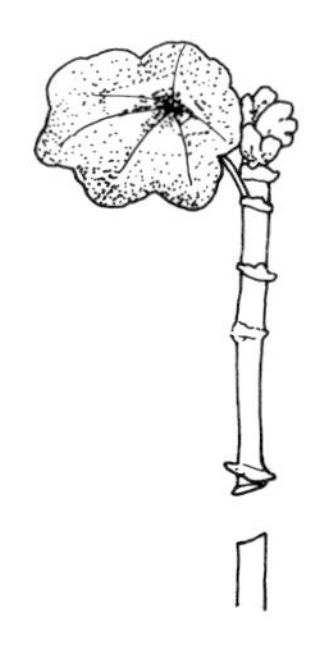

Taking a soft cutting, just below the node

and there is no point in using excess. If the base of the cutting is dipped about ½in. (1cm) into the powder and is then tapped lightly against the top of the container, the right amount should adhere, even to an unmoistened cutting. The dilutant is talc, and it is so finely divided that it will stick firmly.

Only the large-leaved rhododendrons require rooting hormones at higher concentrations and, as these are very difficult to strike anyway for the amateur, one should try for the perfect technique rather than for the perfect hormone!

Leafy cuttings are of two kinds: soft and half-ripe. A soft cutting is one that is taken, usually early in the year, when the growth is young and pliable, so that it can be freely bent without snapping. Soft cuttings can be taken from many shrubs, from a very large number of alpines and from herbaceous plants.

Soft cuttings are very prone to wilting, so they should be put into a plastic bag as soon as they are removed from the plant and there should be as little delay in preparing them and getting them into their new humid home as possible. This applies especially to herbaceous cuttings taken in summer, such as penstemons and pelargoniums, and to the very small and extremely soft tip cuttings from alpines. These will often root extremely quickly, especially if placed in a south-facing frame with net shading and frequent spraying. I have rooted an alpine phlox inside five days!

Soft cuttings are also vulnerable to attack by fungi and it is good practice to soak each one in a fungicide solution. By 'soak' I do not mean that they be given a long languid bath, but that they should be completely immersed.

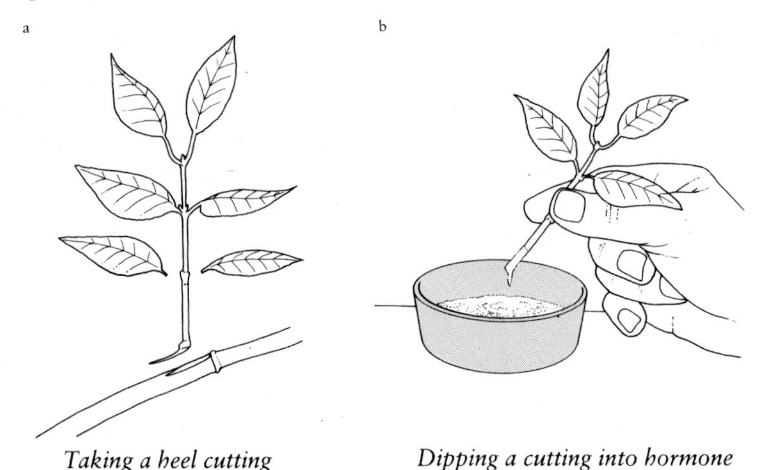

Taking a heel cutting

Dipping a cutting into hormone rooting powder

Some cuttings are taken from growth that is so short that nodal cuttings are impossible. An example of this is the alpine thrift, *Armeria caespitosa*, which is a tight bun of very short stems with minute needle-like leaves. Here, the new soft growth can be gently pulled away downwards so that a heel – a short sliver of the old stem – comes away with it. This is trimmed up before the cutting is inserted. Heel cuttings are the best way of dealing with plants with hollow or pithy stems and are often the only method by which some shrubs can be propagated.

Half-ripe cuttings are a little difficult to define, as the condition of half-ripeness is not an exact one. When a new shoot on a shrub has reached its full length, its tissues will start to become progressively woody, until, by the end of the summer in most cases, they are rigid and will snap if an attempt is made to bend them. At a half-way stage in this process, the shoot may be bent without snapping only to about 20 degrees from the vertical and its tip will have become firm and solid,

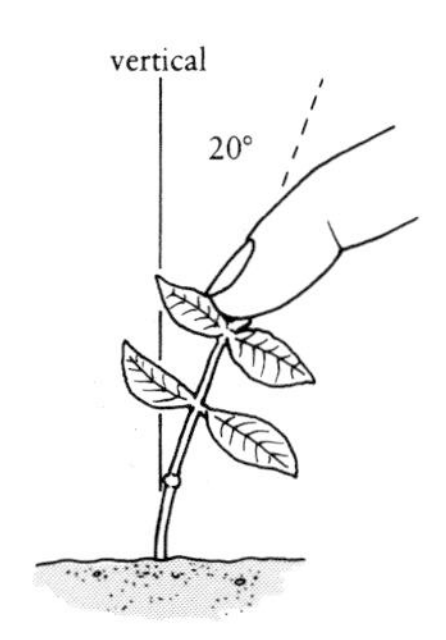

Testing a half-ripe shoot before taking a cutting

instead of rather floppy. A shoot in this condition is right for being taken as a cutting and it will not be as likely to wilt as a soft cutting.

There are other reasons why many people (myself included) prefer to take shrub cuttings at the half-ripe stage. They are, generally, much easier to handle and to look after; they do not succumb nearly as readily to fungal attacks, and they have bigger food reserves and do not need to root as quickly. Furthermore, as many shrubs have leaves that are adapted against water loss, and often those adaptations, such as the thick skins of camellia leaves, do not develop until the shoot begins to mature, the cuttings are altogether safer.

Most softwood cuttings can be potted up relatively early in the year as soon as they have developed good root systems. This applies to a lot of half-ripe ones as well, but it is often a good idea to leave those that root in the latter part of the summer or in the autumn until the following spring before they are potted. Some plants, including evergreen azaleas, *Crinodendron* and *Eucryphia*, will almost certainly die if an attempt is made to pot them in the year they are taken, and the rule is that if you are in doubt, leave them until the spring. They will be perfectly all right without any covering other than that of an airy frame and with the occasional watering, and they will need no feeding.

Leafy cuttings can be assisted by several relatively modern improvements in propagation methods, but only two are of real interest to most gardeners. Mist propagation is within the reach of the greenhouse owner who takes a lot of cuttings. This consists of an automatic atomising spray governed by a device which senses dryness in the atmosphere and activates a short burst of fine droplets of water over the cuttings. Some systems are better than others, but all have the advantage that the cuttings need no shading and root a good deal more quickly than with conventional methods. Difficult cuttings, too, are rendered much easier, and the overall percentage strike is much higher. The amateur who is thinking of installing one of the smaller mist systems that are available should consult a professional who knows about the pros and cons of the various kinds on the market.

Mist is always used with bottom heat in the form of cables or of a new product which consists of a conductive ink ducted within a plastic sheet. Bottom heat greatly increases rooting and should be used wherever possible, with or without a mist system. The great advantage

GENUS OR SPECIES?

The system of plant classification used in this country is the same as that used all over the world. It is in Latin, a form of international language.

Plants are classified according to family, genus, species and variety.

The genus is equivalent to a surname and is given to a group of plants that are broadly similar in structure and are thought to have a common ancestor.

When a plant's full name is given, the genus name is always first – for example, *Solidago*. *Solidago* is a member of a group of related plants, called the family, which in this case is *Compositae*, a family to which chrysanthemums also belong. The genus is the basic unit and may include a number of species with similar structures – golden rod (*Solidago virgaurea*), for instance, has a North American form called *Solidago canadensis*; *virgaurea* and *canadensis* are the species names.

If variations occur naturally within a species, these can be subdivided into varieties and they are usually given a Latin name; but if the variety has been cultivated by hybridisation, the variety name is in English, as in the following example:

Family	**Genus**	**Species**	**Variety**
Compositae	*Solidago*	*canadensis*	'Gardeners' World'

of the conductive ink idea is that the heat is very even and the sheet can be rolled up and stored in a small space when it is not wanted. Soil heating cables are good, but need to be replaced after a few years, as they tend to develop fractures which stop them working.

HARDWOOD CUTTINGS

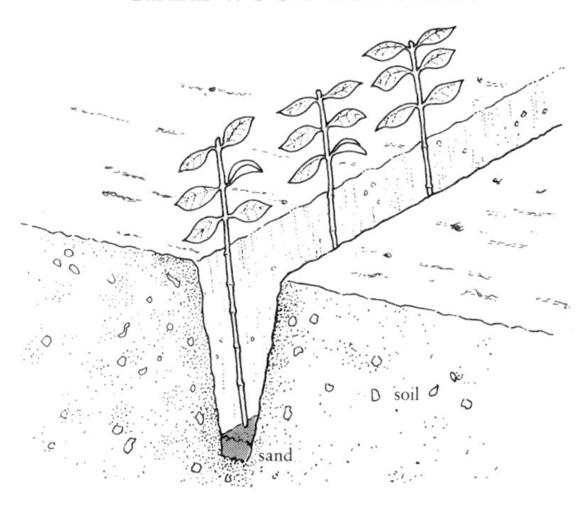

Rooting hardwood cuttings in a trench

Non-leafy (or hardwood) cuttings are as simple as apple pie. Lengths of hard stems from the current year's growth are taken in autumn after leaf-fall and cut into pieces from 4 to 14in. (10 to 35.5cm) in length, depending on the source. They are taken at a node, but the real essential is that there should be a bud at the top from which new growth will start. Rooting does not happen at the node, but from the cambium (a layer under the bark), so the cuttings are inserted deeply, two thirds of their length being below ground. They are placed vertically in trenches in fairly shady places in the open, and many will have rooted by the late spring or early summer following. There is, of course, no need to cover them, as you will have remembered that it is leaves that lose water and they do not have any.

Those who take cactus cuttings may well curse my opening remarks about the urge for survival, as they appear to disobey the rules and refuse to root. The same applies to succulents. The thinking gardener will, however, realise that such a cutting, laden with water and adapted to prolonged drought, does not know that it is under threat. Leave it lying on the bench for a few days, though, until it starts to wrinkle, and it will have had such a scare thrown into it that it will demonstrate its will to live by rooting faster than anything else.

CONTROL OF PESTS AND DISEASES
Insecticides

Chemical	Brand Name	Pest
Bacillus Thuringiensis Berliner	Herbon Thuricide HP	Caterpillars
Borax	Nippon Ant Destroyer Liquid	Ants
Bromophos	Bromophos	Wireworm Carrot fly etc.
Carbaryl	Murphy Lawn Pest Killer Murphy Wasp Destroyer	Worms Leather jackets
Diazinon	Root Guard	Soil pests
Dimethoate	Boots Greenfly and Blackfly Killer Murphy Systemic Insecticide	Greenfly Blackfly Thrips Leafhoppers
Dimethoate and Pyrethrin	Bio Long Last	All garden pests
Fenitrothion	Murphy Fentro pbi Fenitrothion	Caterpillars Leafhoppers Codling moth Sawfly
Gamma BHC	Boots Ant Destroyer Fumite Loft Guard Smoke May and Baker Greenhouse Smoke Murphy Ant Killer Powder Murphy Gamma BHC	All soil pests Ants Aphids Woodworm
Malathion	Malathion Greenfly Killer Murphy Greenhouse Aerosol Murphy Liquid Malathion Murphy Malathion Dust	Aphids Thrips Leafhoppers Caterpillars

Insecticides

Chemical	Brand Name	Pest
Permethrin	Bio Fly Down Bio Spray Day Boots Caterpillar and Whitefly Killer Fisons Whitefly and Caterpillar Killer Fumite Whitefly Smoke House Plant Leafshine plus Pest Killer May and Baker Greenhouse Smoke Whitefly Killer Murphy Whitefly Smoke Picket	Aphids Whitefly Caterpillars etc.
Permethrin/ Heptenophos	Murphy Tumblebug	All major plant pests
Permethrin/ Malathion	Crop Saver	All major vegetable pests
Pirimicarb	Abol G Rapid Greenfly Killer Rapid Aerosol	Aphids
Pirimiphos Methyl	Fumite Greenhouse Insecticide Smoke ICI Antkiller Sybol 2 Sybol 2 Dust	Ants Aphids Caterpillars
Pyrethrum	Anti Ant Duster Big Gun	Ants Aphids Leafhoppers Caterpillars
Resmethrin	House Plant Pest Killer Burts House Plant Pesticide	Aphids Caterpillars
Rotenone (Derris)	Abol Derris Dust Corrys Derris Dust Liquid Derris Murphy Derris Dust	Aphids Caterpillars

Fungicides

Chemical	Brand Name	Pest
Benomyl	Benlate	Black spot Mildew Cane spot Fusarium
Bupirimate/ Triforin	Nimrod T Roseclear (also insecticide)	Rust Black spot Mildew
Captan and Gamma BHC	Murphy Combined Seed Dressing	Damping off
Carbendazim	Boots Garden Fungicide	Mildew Black spot Botrytis
Copper Compound	Corrys Bordeaux Mixture Murphy Liquid Copper Fungicide	Rusts Vine mildew Downy mildew
Copper Sulphate Ammonium Carbonate	Cheshunt Compound	Damping off
Fenarimol	Fisons Mildew and Black Spot Killer	Mildew Black spot
Mancozeb	Dithane 945	Rust Potato blight etc.
Calomel	pbi Calomel Dust ICI Club Root Control	Club root
Tecnazine	May and Baker Greenhouse Disease Killer Fumite Tecnalin Smoke Murphy Pest and Disease Smoke	Mildew Botrytis
Thiophanate	Fungus Fighter Liquid Club Root Control Murphy Systemic Club Root Dip Murphy Systemic Fungicide	Mildew Black spot Club root Cane spot

Herbicides

Chemical	Brand Name	Weeds Treated
Alloxydim Sodium	Weed Out	Couch grass
Aminotriazole	Fisons Path Spot Weedkiller Super Weedex Fisons Path Weedkiller	All weeds
2, 4-D and Dicamba	Fisons Lawn Spot Weedkiller Weedgun	Lawn weeds
2, 4-D Dicamba/ Ioxynil	Bio Lawn Weedkiller Super Verdone	Lawn weeds
2, 4-D and Dichlorprop and Mecoprop	Boots Lawn Weedkiller	Lawn weeds
Dalapon	Couch and Grass Killer Herbon Dalapon	Couch grass
Dichlorophen	Bio Moss Killer Murphy Super Moss Killer Mosslox-Plus	Moss
Glyphosate	Murphy Tumbleweed	Perennial weeds
Ioxynil	Actrilawn New Lawns Weedkiller	Lawn weeds
Ioxynil and Mecoprop	New Clovercide Extra Lawn Weedspray New Clovotox	Clovers
Paraquat and Diquat	Weedol	Annuals
Paraquat/ Diquat/ Simazine Aminotriazole	Pathclear	All weeds
Propachlor	Murphy Covershield Weed Preventer	Emergent weeds
Simazine	Weedex	All weeds

THE WORRY OF WEEDS

BY CLAY JONES

By definition, a weed is any plant that is growing where it shouldn't. In gardening terms, we regard weeds as those native wild plants that insist on invading places where we wish to grow plants of our choice. In the not too distant past, weed eradication was purely physical. We tackled them by hand or hoe, but in recent years a wide selection of chemical weedkillers (herbicides) has eased the chore of weed control and taken much of the backache out of weeding. (Readers who believe that chemicals should be used sparingly in the garden, if at all, should see 'A Basic Guide to Organic Gardening' by Geoff Hamilton on page 70.)

Weeds fall into two main categories: annuals and perennials. Annual weeds such as bittercress, groundsel and shepherd's purse exist as plants for only one growing season. At the end of it they die, and they ensure the survival of their kind by leaving behind their seeds. These lie dormant in the soil over winter and germinate in the spring to reinfect the whole garden. Therefore, one method of controlling them is to prevent them from seeding; to kill them before they flower. The old adage 'One year's seeding, seven years' weeding' still holds good. In the vegetable garden and in flower beds regular hoeing when the weeds are just past the seedling stage is still the best way of dealing with the annual kinds, but remember to use a sharp hoe and use it on a dry, sunny day, so that the severed and uprooted weeds wilt quickly and perish.

Perennial weeds are more persistent and are the very devil to eradicate. They can survive chopping with a hoe and even some herbicides, by virtue of their underground organs. Some have long thick tap roots, others have ramifying rhizomes, all capable of regenerating new growth. In fact, many of them will produce new and complete plants from quite small pieces of root. This explains why rotovating an area of weed-infested ground usually results in an even more prolific population of perennial weeds than previously, and why it is pointless screwing off the leaves of dandelions, leaving their roots in the ground – they only grow again.

To kill them physically, such weeds have to be dug up without leaving a vestige of root behind. Alternatively, you can smother them to death by covering the area for a season with black polythene or even an old piece of foam-backed carpet. It excludes light, the life-giving force,

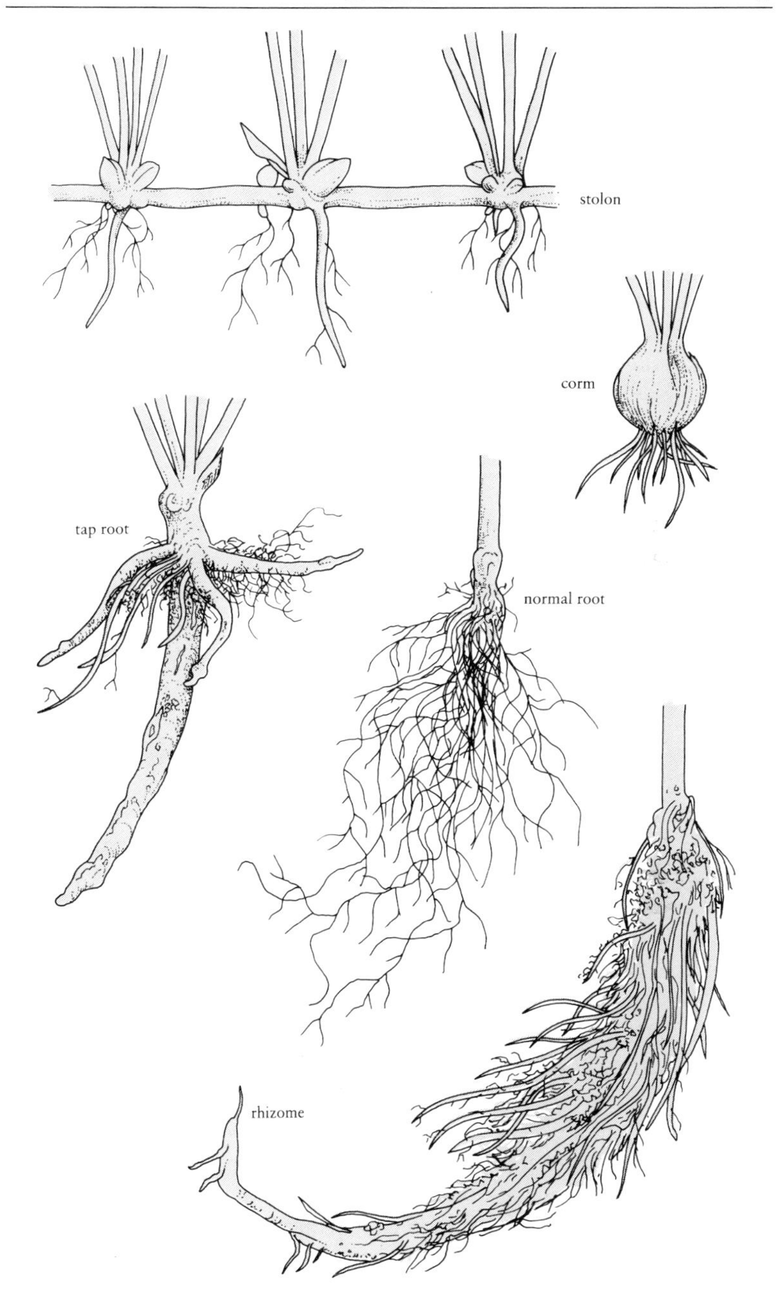

Types of root commonly found on weeds:
stolon (e.g. creeping buttercup), corm (e.g. oxalis), tap root (e.g. dandelion), normal root (e.g. shepherd's purse), rhizome (e.g. bindweed)

and the weeds die of starvation. If you hate the sight of black polythene or a carpeted garden, try mulching in between your cultivated plants with a 3 to 4in. (7.5 to 10cm) layer of peat or pulverised bark. It will suppress most annual weeds but, being persistent, most of the perennials will push their way up through it. I have known dandelions drill their way upwards through solid concrete and untreated tarmac holds no fears for them, and this is when I say, 'Hooray for the chemical herbicides!' They are, without doubt, the greatest boon that has befallen gardeners since Adam found apples to his liking, but they must be handled with care and used correctly and sparingly.

One of the earliest chemical herbicides was sodium chlorate, still available but largely superseded by its betters. Its major disadvantages are its prolonged persistence in the soil and its tendency to permeate beyond desired limits. Treated soil can remain toxic to plants for a year or more and, unless one is very careful, precious plants in ground adjacent to a treated area may be killed.

The mixture of the herbicides paraquat and diquat, sold under the name of Weedol, will effectively eradicate all green growth above soil level, but it has no effect on plant roots. It will totally kill all annual weeds and it is the ideal herbicide to apply in spring as weed growth starts to push through the soil. It is non-persistent, and therefore treated ground may be planted within a few days of application. Unfortunately, it is also lethal to humans, even in very small doses, so treat it with the utmost respect.

The chemical simazine is a persistent weedkiller, but as it goes into suspension rather than into solution in water, it has specific uses. It is of value in keeping paths and drives clear of weeds for a whole season, and as it penetrates to only just below the soil surface, it can be used as a pre-emergence weedkiller on beds containing deep-rooted plants such as trees and shrubs. It follows that simazine is at its most effective when applied in early spring, before weeds are evident. It is sold under the brand names of Weedex and Pathclear among others.

The gold medal for herbicides must be awarded to the remarkable systemic herbicide glyphosate, to be found on the shelves as Tumbleweed. This gardeners' friend enters plants via the leaves, travels through the conducting system right down to the deepest roots and kills the whole plant. One snag, if it is a snag, is its tardiness. Its fatal effects may not be noticeable for three weeks or more from application; but be patient – it works a treat. I have used it with total success to kill such previously imperishable things as ground elder, bindweed, nettles and even old man's beard. Tumbleweed is expensive but less costly to use if you apply it with a sprayer rather than with a watering can. It kills all green plants, so keep it off those you prize, but it is non-persistent and treated ground can be planted up within a few days of application.

Couch grass, twitch or scutch, call it what you will, is a perennial nuisance, especially when it finds its way into rockeries and the bases of hedges. Fortunately, the chemical alloxydim sodium is a specific couch grass herbicide. It kills no other plants, so you can use it with confidence wherever the weed is growing in close association with cultivated plants.

Finally, there are the lawn weedkillers that eradicate flat-leaved weeds, including docks, daisies and dandelions, without harming the grass. They are available in both granular and liquid form, and of the two I prefer to use the liquids. Their effect is faster, they do not rely on rain to wash them into the leaves and the family pets can walk on the grass as soon as it is dry without suffering any ill effects.

My last word on the subject of pesticides is to stress that they are invaluable gardening aids when they are used strictly in accordance with the manufacturers' instructions. Used without the necessary diligence, they can be lethal to humans, pets and wild life. Furthermore, it is pointless using a herbicide at anything other than the recommended dilution. A weedkiller applied at double strength will not annihilate the weeds twice as fast or twice as effectively; it will just cost twice as much!

BUDGET IDEAS

- Use plastic bottles with the bottom cut off as propagators.
- Use yoghurt cartons as plant pots. Make holes in the bottom for drainage.
- Go to demolition contractors for second-hand bricks and timber.
- Go to the Post Office sorting office for short lengths of string.
- For second-hand tools, go to house clearance auctions and car boot sales.
- Join a gardening society and buy fertilisers and so on in bulk.
- Be forward-looking and grow your perennials from seed.
- If you do buy plants, buy just one: you can divide it or take cuttings and have more next year.
- Don't spend money on weedkillers if you have only a small garden. Use a hoe or your hands.

A BASIC GUIDE TO ORGANIC GARDENING

BY GEOFF HAMILTON

With an increased concern for healthy food and for the environment, organic gardening has really taken off.

As more garden chemicals previously thought to be harmless are withdrawn from garden centres, the demand for safer cultivation methods grows. Many gardeners are now looking for an alternative, so with that in mind, I have, for several years now, been investigating organic methods on our trial ground at Barnsdale. The aim has been to discover whether or not organic gardening works and how much extra it costs in terms of time and money.

While I would not suggest that the trials have been strictly scientific, comparisons of several different methods have consistently shown that the organic way produces equal yields with far less damage from pests and diseases than I at first thought likely. The labour commitment is probably slightly higher, but our costings have shown that it need not be more expensive. Indeed, in most years the organic plots proved cheaper.

WHAT IS 'ORGANIC'?

Considerable confusion is caused by the terms 'organic' and 'chemical'. Of course, all things on earth are made up of chemicals, including all so-called 'non-chemical' organic pesticides and fertilisers. By the same token, it does not necessarily follow that because a chemical is plant- or animal-derived it must be safe. Think of belladonna or heroin!

However, organic gardeners do not suggest that their pesticides will kill nothing but the 'baddies' nor that plants will take up their nutrients in any different form because they happen to be organically derived. What they do say is that nature's own methods of pest and disease control and of supplying plant nutrients will be more sympathetic to the soil and to the garden and its resident community of wild life.

And, perhaps most important, the food we eat will, because we have grown it ourselves and know what has gone into it, be guaranteed free from synthetic chemicals.

Of course, while organic gardeners employ natural methods, they recognise that we demand far, far more from our soil than nature ever intended. While a square yard of soil in the wild might, for example, produce little more than a couple of thin, tough wild carrots, we expect the same area to yield a dozen or more fat, juicy specimens for the table.

So, in a nutshell, the organic way is to use nature's own methods of growing – but more so.

THE SOIL

The organic gardener's approach to the management of the soil differs considerably from that of the purely chemical grower. The influence of the majority of commercial growers and farmers has persuaded many modern gardeners to adopt the same highly successful chemical methods. For these people the principle is that the soil is used solely as a means of anchoring roots and holding water and nutrients, and the plant is then 'force-fed' with the minerals it requires. The method works well, but at high cost.

First, the use of high levels of chemicals in the soil has been shown to cause serious pollution problems. But perhaps even more damaging in the long run is the fact that, without organic matter to improve its structure, the soil becomes poorly drained, airless and difficult to cultivate. What's more, without the life-giving organic matter they need, the beneficial soil organisms simply die out.

And there is a further complication. Feeding plants with an excess of artificial fertiliser, especially nitrogen, causes soft, sappy growth which is prone to attack from pests and diseases. So the chemical grower resorts to poisonous sprays to get rid of them – sprays which the organic gardener rarely needs. Once locked into the chemical system, it's difficult to escape.

The organic gardener, on the other hand, believes in feeding the soil rather than the plant, just as would happen in nature. By adding high levels of bulky organic matter in the form of manure, garden compost and so on, he or she aims to form a highly fertile soil which will support a thriving soil life, retain water and nutrients and which will be well

WHAT IS HUMUS?

Humus is a vital ingredient in any soil. Soil that has no humus is nothing more than ground-up rock, and as such cannot hold water or plant nutrients. Humus is thoroughly decayed plant and animal matter which, through bacterial action, has been transformed into something known as a 'colloidal gum'. This substance not only provides a cement to join the soil particles into a good structure, but also in itself contains valuable nutrients in a readily available form for plants to take up.

drained enough to permit the free passage of air and of plant roots. The plants will then be able to remove water and nutrients as and when they want them. This approach results in a stronger plant, generally more able to resist attacks from pests and diseases.

ORGANIC MATTER

The main plank of the organic gardener's soil-management technique, therefore, is organic matter. There are several alternative sources.

Manure

If you live in the country where farmers run cows or horses, supplies of farmyard manure are generally plentiful and relatively cheap. It's the very best form of organic matter, being high in nutrients, and a fine soil conditioner.

Of course, compared with chemical fertilisers, the nutrient levels seem very low indeed. An average sample of cow manure, for example, contains only 0.6% nitrogen, 0.3% phosphate and 0.5% potash. Compared with Growmore at 7% of each, it seems a poor source of nutrients. Remember, though, that you'll be using a far greater volume of manure than fertiliser. What's more, apart from the nutrient value, it will also greatly improve the soil structure.

While farmyard manure is difficult to come by if you live in an urban area, horse muck is often freely available. Even large towns have their riding stables which are very often only too pleased to sell the manure quite cheaply.

Always stack animal manures for at least a year. Used fresh they will be strong enough to scorch young roots and stems and will almost certainly contain impurities.

Spent Mushroom Compost

A waste product from the mushroom-growing industry, spent compost can be an excellent source of organic matter, though it does have its limitations. It consists of horse manure which has been composted and mixed with peat and ground chalk to grow a crop of mushrooms. It is then discarded and sold, either in bags straight from the mushroom farm, or in bales from garden centres. It is generally fairly easy to obtain, even in urban areas.

Spent mushroom compost makes a good soil conditioner for the vegetable garden, though its nutrient content is relatively low. Its main drawback is that the chalk in it will alter the acidity of the soil, and for this reason it should rarely be used round ornamental plants and never round acid lovers like rhododendrons, azaleas, heathers or pieris.

Again, stack it for a year before use.

Other Alternatives

Peat is a bit of a last resort for the serious organic gardener, since it is very expensive and contains few or no nutrients. It is, however, an excellent soil conditioner.

Seaweed makes a very good soil improver and will also add nutrients but, naturally, is limited in supply to coastal areas. It contains a very wide range of the so-called trace elements essential to plant growth but needed only in minute quantities.

Spent hops, which come from the brewing industry, are also useful but are difficult to come by these days since most are removed from breweries under contract for processing.

Wool shoddy, which consists of bits of fluffy wool, can sometimes be bought in wool-processing areas. It makes an excellent soil conditioner and can be dug wet into the soil in autumn.

Compost

One of the best and certainly the cheapest of all soil conditioners is home-made compost. No garden, organic or chemical, should be without its compost heap, which can be used to turn all the vegetable waste from the garden and the kitchen into a superb soil conditioner, relatively rich in plant nutrients.

The best way to make compost is in a container or, as in most organic gardens, several containers. There are plenty available at garden centres but it's very easy and much cheaper to make your own. It con-

Stacking compost in alternating layers of fine and coarse material

sists simply of a wooden box with a removable front to give access to the rotted compost.

Fill the container with anything that is going to rot down – grass cuttings, weeds, vegetable waste from the garden and the kitchen, newspaper cut into shreds, old woollen or cotton clothing and so on. There is only one point to bear in mind when stacking it. To work properly, the bacteria which do the job of rotting down the compost need air, so avoid using fine vegetable matter (such as grass cuttings), which tends to exclude air, on its own. Either stack it in 6in. (15cm) layers with a layer of coarser material between, or mix it with weeds or other vegetable matter.

The process will be accelerated if you remove and replace the compost after a month or so in the summer, to re-aerate it. It's also a good idea to keep the heap covered with a bit of old carpet or sacking to prevent it from losing too much heat, for this too will slow down the activity of the bacteria.

Some gardeners also add an accelerator, but I find that it is not entirely necessary. If you do favour it, use seaweed meal.

Of course, it's impossible to find all you need from the garden and house to supply enough compost for the whole garden. You might therefore have to go out and collect extra organic matter – perhaps from the greengrocer, who throws away mountains of waste, or the cricket or golf club, which will often have excess grass cuttings.

Leaf Mould

Leaf mould is an ideal material for use as a peat substitute, but it should be noted that leaves are rotted down in a different way. It's mainly fungi that do the work here, so stack leaves separately from compost. A

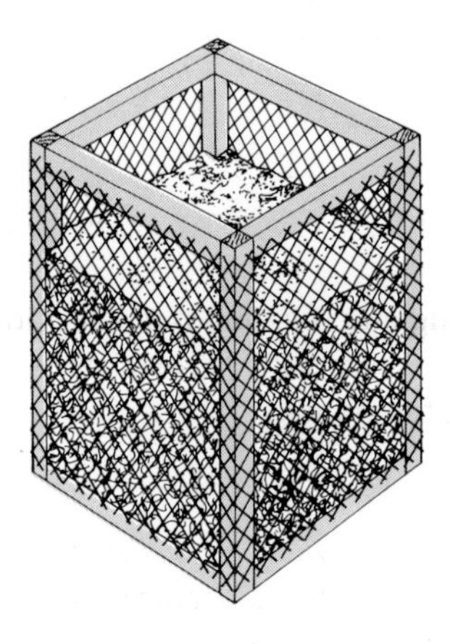

Making leaf mould

simple wire-netting cage will suffice. Some local councils are happy to provide leaves to supplement your own supply.

Worms

Worms can be employed to rot down compost and manure more quickly than bacteria, and to improve the product in the process. The material passes through the body of the worm where it is coated in a gel and ejected in pellet form. The resulting crumb structure helps to improve drainage and aeration. The action of the worm also makes the plant nutrients readily available to roots but in a slow-release form so that it can be drawn on as and when required.

The simplest way to make your own wormery is to drill several holes in the bottom of a small dustbin and rest it on a couple of bricks. That's all there is to it.

The worms you need are a special type called brandlings, and they're generally available from fishing tackle shops. Put them into a 'starter'

Making worm compost

of rotted compost and then pile a layer of green compost material on top. They'll soon work through it and it can be added to until the bin is full. Then sieve the compost to remove the worms and start again. The worms won't live in soil, so use them only for compost.

The resulting material can be used in sowing and potting composts with great success. I have found the best mix to be 25% worm compost and 75% peat for sowing and half and half for potting. Use it also as a 'starter' sprinkled down seed drills before sowing, or as a nutritious mulch around ornamental plants.

Green Manure

If you have a large garden or work an allotment, green manuring can be a useful way of adding organic matter to the soil. Many green manure plants are legumes, which have the ability to manufacture nitrogen in nodules in their roots. When the plants are cut down and dug in, the nitrogen is released and made available.

Choose a crop that will mature in the time you require and sow in rows or broadcast over the soil surface. Cut it down at the appropriate time, allow it to wilt for a while and then dig it in, burying it no more than about 6in (15cm) deep.

Suitable Plants for Green Manure

Alfalfa (Lucerne) Sow in spring and dig in during autumn, or sow in late summer and dig in during spring.
Broad bean Sow in autumn and dig in during spring.
Red clover Sow in spring or later summer and dig in when the land is required.
Winter tares Sow in late summer and dig in during spring.
Rye Sow in late summer and dig in during spring.
Phacelia Sow in summer and dig in eight weeks later.
Mustard Sow in spring and summer and dig in before flowering.

FERTILISERS

If you can find enough manure, fertilisers will not be necessary. Generally, however, gardeners need to use a certain amount to supplement their organic matter.

The main difference between organic and chemical fertilisers is that organic materials are derived from either plant or animal sources or from naturally occurring rock. Nothing is manufactured in the laboratory. Plants require six major elements: nitrogen, phosphorus, potassium and, in rather lower amounts, magnesium, calcium and sulphur. They also need a range of minor (or trace) elements, which will generally be present in fertile soils in sufficient quantities. (See 'Plant Foods and Plant Feeding' by Stefan Buczacki on page 36 for an explanation of the functions of these elements.)

If you use manure or compost, you'll certainly be adding enough trace elements, but the major ones may have to be added 'out of the bag'.

The most popular 'general' fertiliser for supplying the major elements is blood, fish and bonemeal, which is suitable for use all round the garden.

Seaweed meal is widely available and, though more expensive than blood, fish and bone, it contains a better balance of nutrients. Again, it is an excellent general-purpose fertiliser.

Dried animal manures are available but they are slightly lower in major nutrients. They will, however, supply a full range of trace elements.

The three main elements – nitrogen, phosphorus and potassium –

can be supplied as 'straight' fertilisers and are useful either to correct a deficiency or where there is a specific requirement. Bonemeal, for example, is widely used at planting time because it supplies a high level of phosphate which will encourage root growth.

Potash is sometimes supplied in the form of rock potash, to encourage flowering and fruiting, while hoof and horn and dried blood are both valuable sources of nitrogen to encourage leaf and shoot growth.

PEST, DISEASE AND WEED CONTROL

Perhaps the most controversial area of organic gardening, the control of pests and diseases, is riddled with myth and folklore. However, my own experiments have shown that there certainly are effective alternatives to poisonous chemicals.

A Healthy Garden

The first rule in any garden, organic or not, should be to keep it clean, tidy and weed-free. This will remove many alternative hosts of pests and diseases and deprive them of their hiding places. The practice of feeding the soil rather than the plant will encourage strong growth which is more likely to resist attack and which is less attractive to pests and diseases. But you should still be vigilant, ruthlessly removing weak or unhealthy plants and taking off leaves which show signs of attack.

Keep an eye open for the first attack of pests like greenfly or caterpillars. The simple practice of squashing the first few invaders will often avert a full-scale onslaught.

Make sure that you start off with healthy plants. Reject any that show obvious signs of attack or which are not growing strongly. Some plants, particularly fruit and vegetables, are covered by a government scheme which certifies them free from disease. Most fruit trees and bushes are covered, as are potatoes, and you should always ensure when you buy them that a certificate has been issued.

Plant breeders have played an important part in pest and disease control and there are now many varieties of fruit, vegetables and flowers which have pest or disease resistance bred into them. They are an obvious choice for organic gardeners.

Finally, try to avoid varieties notoriously prone to attack. Growing Cox's orange pippin apples or a Frensham rose, for example, is certain to attract mildew which will then spread to other varieties.

Physical Methods of Control

Many pests can be controlled with physical barriers. A wire-netting fence is certainly the best way to deter rabbits, for instance, while a complete covering of netting is the only effective deterrent for birds.

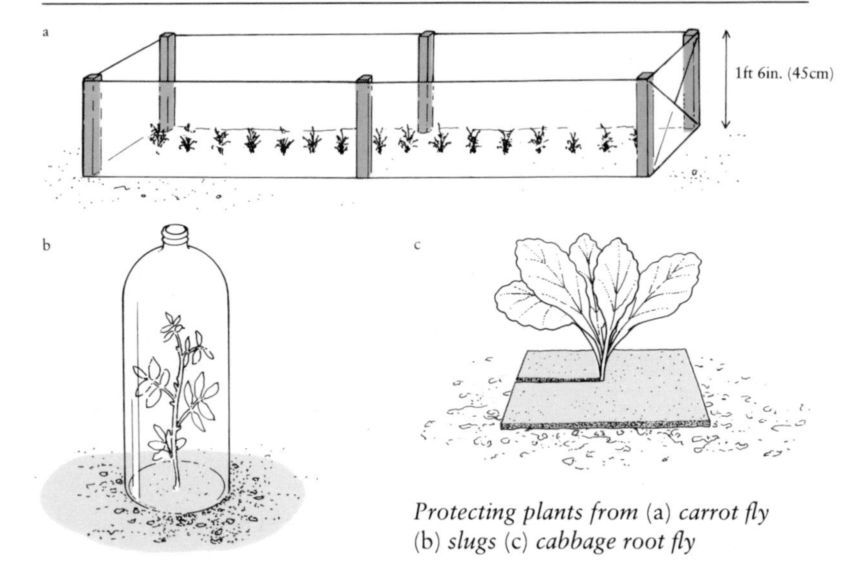

Protecting plants from (a) *carrot fly* (b) *slugs* (c) *cabbage root fly*

Cabbage root fly can be prevented by surrounding plants with a small square of foam rubber carpet underlay. Normally the female lays her eggs right next to the cabbage stem. If she's prevented from doing so by the foam rubber, she'll fly off and find someone else's cabbages!

To reduce attacks by carrot fly, you can grow the crop inside a polythene barrier (as shown in the illustration above). The female flies just above ground level looking for carrots on which to lay her eggs. When she meets the barrier she has to rise above the crop which she then generally flies right over. This method has been found to reduce damage by about 80%.

Slugs can be prevented from attacking young plants by surrounding those vulnerable to attack with a cut-off plastic lemonade bottle. Larger plants may be protected with a 1 gallon (4.5 litre) plastic container similarly treated.

Traps

Many pests can be trapped and destroyed. Slugs, for example, are attracted to beer traps – simply sink a few plastic coffee cups in the soil so that the rims are at ground level and fill them with beer. They fall in and die a glorious death!

Wireworms can be attracted by spiking a piece of potato on to a stick and burying it near the crop with the stick protruding from the soil. They are attracted to the cut potato which can be dug up from time to time and the wireworms destroyed. Alternatively, buy a little corn from the pet shop and sow a row near vulnerable crops. The wire-

Slug trap – plastic coffee cup filled with beer

Earwig trap – upturned flower pot filled with dried grass

worms prefer corn roots which can be later dug up and destroyed.

Flea beetles attack young seedlings, especially brassicas, making numerous small round holes. They are called flea beetles because of their habit of jumping when approached and this can be used to control them. Coat a small piece of wood or hardboard with old grease. Pass it over the top of the affected crop and the beetles will jump upwards and stick to the grease.

Earwigs attack plants like dahlias and chrysanthemums, chewing and distorting buds. They don't like daylight, so provide them with a hiding place by filling a flower pot with dried grass and fixing it, upturned, to the top of a stick near the plants you wish to protect. The earwigs will crawl in during the day when they can be removed and destroyed.

Greenhouse whitefly are attracted to anything yellow, so hang up a yellow card covered with light grease. You will find that they fly on to it and stick fast.

The larvae of codling moths attack apples, burrowing into the young fruit and feeding inside. They can be reduced by about 80% with a pheromone trap, available inexpensively from garden centres. It consists of a plastic 'tent' inside which is placed a sticky pad. A capsule containing the pheromone – the chemical excreted by the female fly at mating time to attract males – is put in the middle of the pad and attracts male moths which stick to it. With no fertilisation there are, of course, no larvae to feed on the apples.

Natural Controls

In the organic garden much use is made of nature's own controls. Predators can be attracted by growing a wide diversity of plants, to provide food and shelter. The hoverfly, for example, needs a feed of pollen before laying her eggs. Since she has a short feeding tube she requires open flowers like French marigolds or convolvulus. After feeding, she lays her eggs in clusters of aphids which the resulting larvae eat by the thousand.

Ground beetles feed on many insect pests, including aphids and caterpillars. They require a hiding place during the day and can be encouraged by growing ground-covering plants under which they can hide.

Birds are very valuable as pest controllers and they can be attracted by planting trees for perching and nesting and berried plants for food. Make sure you keep the hoe going around the borders to expose soil pests which will soon be spotted by hungry birds.

Biological controls are a relatively new development. They consist of predators of pests which can be artificially introduced into the garden or greenhouse. Many have a limited success in the garden because once the pest is eliminated the predators also die, making it a very expensive exercise. There is one new development, however, which may well

YIELD: FRUIT

Approximate yield you can expect from a fruit tree or bush (figures based on established well-grown specimens):

	Bush		Espalier	
	lb	kg	lb	kg
Apple	60–120	27–54	20–25	9–11
Pear	40–100	18–45	15–20	7–9
Plum	30–60	13.5–27		
Cherry, sweet	30–120	13.5–54		
Cherry, morello	30–40	13.5–18		
Peach	30–60	13.5–27		
Apricot				
Fig				
Blackcurrant	10–13	4.5–6		
Redcurrant	6–12	2.7–5.5		
Gooseberry	8–10	3.6–4.5		

show the way for the future: *Bacillus thuringiensis*, a bacterium which is available in packets, freeze-dried and made into a sprayable powder. If sprayed on caterpillars, it attacks the digestive system, stopping the caterpillars eating and quickly killing them.

Organic Chemicals

As a last resort there are a few plant-derived chemicals which are considered safe. They persist for only one day, so there is little danger to humans, but they can kill garden friends as well as enemies.
Derris is effective against most pests, including caterpillars, but is also harmful to predators and very dangerous to fish.
Insecticidal soap, based on potassium, will control whitefly, aphids, red spider mite, scale insects and mealy bug.
Pyrethrum and *rotenone* will kill most insects and are harmless to animals.
Copper is a permissible fungicide and is sometimes also sold as Bordeaux mixture or Burgundy mixture. It coats the leaves and will stay active against mildews and blights for several weeks, though new foliage will not be protected until sprayed again.
Dispersible sulphur is also allowed, though it should, in my view, be used with care and only as a very last resort.

Fan		Single Cordon		Standard	
lb	kg	lb	kg	lb	kg
12–30	5.5–13.5	5–8	2.2–3.6	100–400	45–181
12–30	5.5–13.5	4–6	2–2.7	80–240	36–108
				30–100	13.5–45
12–30	5.5–13.5			30–120	13.5–54
12–30	5.5–13.5			30–120	13.5–54
12–30	5.5–13.5			30–120	13.5–54
12–30	5.5–13.5			30–120	13.5–54
12–30	5.5–13.5				

Weed Control

Weedkillers are definitely non-organic and should be shunned in the natural garden. The hoe is, in any case, a much better, safer and more effective control.

Another aid used by the organic gardener is to exclude light by mulching between rows of vegetables with black polythene or paper and between ornamental plants with organic matter. Composted bark is a newish material that is both very effective and attractive.

In a new garden that needs clearing of weeds, consider covering the whole plot with black polythene or an old foam-backed carpet at the outset, leaving it for a season and starting clean from day one.

Finally, remember that weeds should never be allowed to flower and seed. There are literally thousands of seeds on one plant which, if allowed to spread, will make life that much harder the following year.

After many years of experimenting, there is no doubt in my mind that, if you are prepared to use sound methods of cultivation and to be meticulous in garden hygiene, you'll grow fine crops and healthy flowers and fruits without ever having to resort to poisonous chemicals.

AUTUMN

AUGUST
SEPTEMBER
OCTOBER

HARDY PLANTS AT BRESSINGHAM
Alan Bloom

A SEED IN TIME
Roy Lancaster

HOUSEPLANTS
Anne Swithinbank

AUGUST

VEGETABLE PATCH

If you are going away on holiday, neighbours can be bribed into watering young plants and tomatoes by being invited to pick courgettes, calabrese, beans and so on. In fact you're not giving anything away, but simply encouraging the plants to produce new young succulent produce that will be ready on your return. Your neighbour, however, will think you generous, and his or her care will hopefully prevent that acute feeling of sadness and neglect that rows of dead seedlings engender.

Where crops have been harvested, sow spinach and Japanese onions. To get extra-long leeks, you can earth them up; it's a must with celery.

Wield the hoe: weeds never stop growing, and a loose dry surface soil helps to prevent loss of water by evaporation.

LAWN

Really dry weather may let you off a bit of mowing. As you should definitely *not* waste water on it, a little neglect will be positively beneficial to the grass as a plant. It just depends how proud you are.

If you are daft enough to want some more lawn, you can grow it from seed this month and next. Fork over the soil and rake down to a fine tilth, removing stones and levelling. Put on 2 or 3oz of Growmore to the square yard (50–75g per square metre) a week before sowing the seed.

FLOWER BEDS & BORDERS

That boring job of dead-heading fading flowers is still worth doing, but some annuals may be getting really tired. Pull them up and transplant some of those wallflowers and sweet William seedlings into the space. Water and feed, and they'll grow into magnificent plants to flower there next spring.

Herbaceous perennials may be at their best,

and that's the time when you may have to admit that they are in the wrong place. They may be too tall or short, a bad colour match with their neighbours, or simply would look much better in another position – there are all sorts of reasons.

Proper gardeners wait till later to move them; the likes of us move them now. Wait till they die back and it's a case of out of sight, out of mind. However, if you move them now, give them the best chance of survival. First dig a generous hole to put them in. A spadeful of compost or peat, with 2oz (50g) of Growmore or bonemeal, should be mixed thoroughly with the soil in the bottom and very well watered. Then dig up the offending plant with as much soil as possible round the roots, place in its new home, firm down well with the heel of the boot and water it in. Keep watering regularly until you are sure it is re-established.

The really brave move roses and shrubs as well, but it might be wiser to write a note about them, stick it up in a prominent place, and delay action for a month or two.

HOUSEPLANTS, WINDOW BOXES, TUBS & TROUGHS

Add hanging baskets to the above list, and they all, apart from houseplants, need water every day. If you are off to Barbados or Blackpool for a fortnight, this will be a real problem. That neighbour who is eating your vegetables is the only answer for the baskets and tubs. Promise him or her a rooted cutting of your best fuchsia and the purple geranium, and hope for the best.

Baskets cannot be overwatered, neither can well-drained tubs, but houseplants can, and it's more than likely that your generous neighbour will be so conscientious that he or she will drown them while you sun yourself on the beach. For houseplants, therefore, it's safer to rig up a temporary watering system from the sink and/or the bath that will keep them alive, and keep your neighbour from poking around

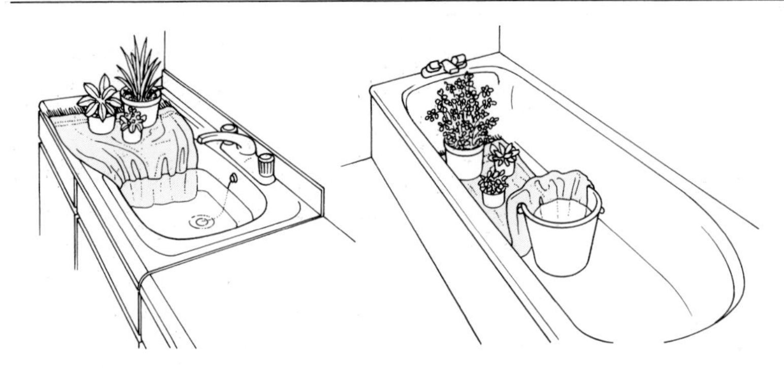

Temporary watering systems

the house! When you get home you may find you've sacrificed two towels, and that the plants are a big leggy because they haven't had as much light as they need, but they will be alive, and your neighbour will not know that the spare bedroom is an awful mess.

FRUIT TREES & BUSHES

Pruning out the wood that carried the flowers on your shrubs is nearly always the right thing to do; similarly with fruit bushes. Raspberry canes that have delivered the goods should be cut down to the ground; other currant bushes (like some shrubs) need more gentle treatment. If you like a particular type, find out from the real experts how to grow it. There are numerous marvellous books in your public library.

Growing good fruit is mostly a matter of the weather at key times of the year, and a bit of basic knowledge. A lot of new growth and not much fruit means a shortage of phosphate. Very little new growth can be cured with nitrogenous fertiliser. Susceptibility to disease probably indicates shortage of potash. Brown edges and spots on leaves indicate shortage of potash and phosphate. As most of us usually forget to feed our fruit trees and bushes, it is not surprising that we are often disappointed. The extraordinary thing is that the old apple tree sometimes produces an enormous crop of perfect fruit.

Common sense suggests fairly frequent applications of a general fertiliser, particularly after the plant has put a lot of energy into producing fruit.

WINDOWSILL, COLD FRAME & GREENHOUSE

That keen gardener up the road will have been picking tomatoes for a month, but you may have only just sampled your first two or three, which taste wonderful. If your plants have six sets of flowers, or trusses, pinch out the top, and make them concentrate on growing them on. They need lots of water, plenty of food and humidity – water the greenhouse floor to help provide this.

Melons will grow a maximum of only six fruits, so being optimistic and greedy is asking too much of the plant. Remove excess flowers and tiny fruits.

Buy some freesia corms and plant in pots for that wonderful scent and beauty in January.

You will probably have numerous pots and trays that have not been cleaned. Fill the dustbin with a strong solution of Jeyes' fluid or Dettol, and soak for twenty-four hours. Rinse well and stack away for next year, or pot up all those rooted cuttings in clean pots.

TREES, SHRUBS & CLIMBERS

Go on taking cuttings from all your favourites, particularly if you know they are tender and might be killed by winter frost.

If you have hedges of any sort, they need to be attacked with vigour. Trimmed now, they will thicken before any cold weather kills off new growth.

By all means try cuttings from clematis, rhododendrons, azaleas, hydrangeas and so on, but a better bet is layering them. Your chances of success are very much greater. Choose a young stem that can be bent down and pinned into the ground with a wire loop. Slice the section that will go into the soil about half-way through, or bend, twist and wound it, then leave it underground until it starts to

Layering a plant

show vigorous growth on the portion beyond the wound. That may take six months or a year. Then transplant. (Page 112 describes how to air-layer a houseplant.)

It is better to start the layering process earlier in the year, as soon as the soil is warm, but August is not too late.

GENERAL

Holidays away from the garden simply exacerbate the problems you already have. Stay at home, do the minimum amount of work, sit and admire your successes, and eat them if appropriate. Gardening is supposed to be fun, not a dreadful responsibility. Philosophers have not dwelt adequately on this dilemma.

HOW MUCH TOP SOIL?

A cubic yard of soil weighs about 1 ton.

WHAT ON EARTH IS A BUSHEL?

A bushel is approximately 8 gallons (36 litres) or four buckets of dry material.

SEPTEMBER

VEGETABLE PATCH

Unless you have a big garden, and grow far more than you can eat, now is the time to ignore the greengrocer and finish off the home-grown vegetables. However, you are unlikely to eat your way through thirty or forty onions, so lift them, let them dry (in the sun if there is any; if not, indoors on newspaper) for a couple of days, then hang them on strings. They look quite decorative, and you snip them off as required.

Potatoes are better dried for a couple of hours in the sun and wind before storing in paper or hessian sacks. Excess carrots and beetroot are well preserved in a box of damp sand, but they also stay fresh buried in perlite. Buying a lot of perlite may seem an unnecessary expense, but you can use it year after year and it is light, enabling you to move the box around with ease, whereas sand is very heavy. (See page 126 for more information on storing vegetables.)

Don't cut the tops off vegetables to be stored: twist them off. If you haven't got any spring cabbage plants of your own, go and buy some now.

Your purple sprouting broccoli plants and Brussels sprouts are liable to get blown about in the wind, which loosens the roots and so diminishes their potential productivity. You can earth up round the roots, or tie them to a cane or firmly planted twig, or both.

LAWN

The time to sow grass seed is now, though a shrub or two, some perennials and ground-cover plants are far more decorative and less work than more lawn. Very small gardens are better with no lawn at all.

Bare patches on your existing lawn should be well scratched with a rake and seeded, then watered frequently.

If you are keen you will scratch the lawn all over with a rake to remove matted growth, and put on lawn fertiliser to build up the plants for the winter.

FLOWER BEDS & BORDERS

Get out those seed packets and read the labels. A good many hardy annuals can be sown now. They will overwinter and flower far earlier than your best efforts in spring with airing cupboard and windowsill.

Beg, borrow or steal a bulb catalogue, and choose a selection of spring-flowering bulbs to set. Apart from the standard crocus and daffodil, there are lovely plants like scillas and aconites. A broad selection will cost a fair bit, so buy a few each year and think carefully about the position that will show them off best. *Don't* plant them too shallow.

Rambling and climbing roses that have finished flowering should have the old wood pruned out and the new tied in. A bit of light and air around new growth helps it mature and flower vigorously next year.

Try collecting seed from annuals before you transfer them to the compost heap. Label the envelopes, or you'll grow a very curious mixture next year.

HOUSEPLANTS, WINDOW BOXES TUBS & TROUGHS

All the spring-flowering bulbs will grow well in pots indoors. If the bowl you choose has no drainage hole, use moist bulb fibre – wet enough to stick together but not so wet that you can squeeze water out of it. The bulbs can be close together, but not touching. Place the planted bowl or pot in a cool, dark, airy place (under the spare bed?) until the leaves are

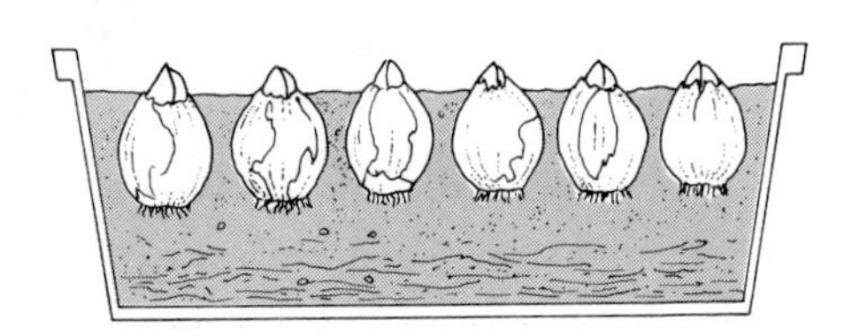

Planting bulbs in a bowl

showing well. Then they need light and warmth.

The garden centre will be stuffed with specially treated bulbs that will flower for Christmas. Try some, and if you haven't already done so, get some untreated (cheaper) bulbs for the trough or window box outside. *Don't* try them if it is very small, however: frost or lack of moisture or something will probably kill them.

Check your houseplants to see if they need re-potting. Don't leave this job any later, because the plant will then not make enough growth to establish itself before winter. If in doubt, wait until the spring.

You would be wise to think of that first frost, and bring indoors tender plants like fuchsias and geraniums. If in pots, leave them there; if not, dig them up, leaving soil round the roots, and stack them in a box. You may need to trim the foliage a bit to get them into the box, but *don't* cut them back. Forget about them until February, when they'll need potting, watering and pruning.

FRUIT TREES & BUSHES

Plant strawberries now, but think carefully before doing so. They are the very devil to keep clear of weeds. The fruit is expensive to buy, however, and home-grown tastes wonderful.

they provide a home for pests over winter.

Finish off pruning currants and, if you have not already done so, cut the old canes of raspberries, blackberries and loganberries right down to the ground, then tie in this year's growth. It provides next year's fruit.

Remember that all fruit likes lime, so if you have not done it earlier, give trees and bushes a dressing now. If you are going to plant new trees later, do a bit of deep digging and mix a generous dollop of lime into the subsoil. It will help the drainage, particularly in heavy soils.

WINDOWSILL, COLD FRAME & GREENHOUSE

If you want to impress the neighbours early next year, sow penstemons, antirrhinums and sweet peas in the cold frame. They will need a bit of protection from heavy frost, so have some polythene and a bit of old carpet handy to put over the top on very cold nights.

Don't leave houseplants on the windowsill at night behind the curtains as they may catch a bad cold. On the other hand, they will like the light during the day.

If your tomato plants are getting tired, remove the remaining fruit to ripen on the windowsill. If the plants are in grow bags, pull them out and replace with strawberry plants.

TREES, SHRUBS & CLIMBERS

Have a good look round the garden centre for a choice climber in a container. The soil in your garden should still be warm enough to encourage the roots to grow into it. Be careful not to let the roots of a newly set plant become dry: a bucket of water a day is not too much. When choosing the plant, make sure that it likes the position in which you intend planting it – a plant that needs a lot of sun, for example, will not be happy if placed against a north-facing wall.

Now is a good time to move evergreen shrubs because the shorter daylight hours and cooler nights reduce the amount of water lost through the leaves (transpiration). They too will need a bucket a day.

Try some cuttings of favourite shrubs (see page 55 for more information on taking cuttings). Put some sand in a narrow trench, poke them in and firm them down.

GENERAL

Choose a nice warm dry evening. Mow the lawn, pour a drink, sit down in a deckchair and contemplate home-grown onions with courgettes, lightly boiled calabrese and blackberry and apple pie for supper.

OCTOBER

VEGETABLE PATCH

If you've been taking any notice of this calendar, you will have late sown carrots and beetroot near or at the eating stage. (They taste better when very small.) Put a cloche over them to encourage that last bit of growth. In fact carrots will stand a little frost, so leave them in the ground. Parsnips and leeks don't need covering, and taste better after they've been frosted.

The digging season is here, so start early, particularly with clay soils; dig a bit at a time, and spread the agony over several weeks. You should have some good compost; dig it in.

LAWN

If your children have been jumping up and down on the grass all year, you really do owe it a bit of effort. Where it has been badly compacted, stick the fork in every few inches and pull gently on the handle to get some air down into the soil and help drainage.

If it is bare between the goal posts, move the posts and re-turf the bald area with bits cut from the left wing. Put the bald bits out on the wing and they'll grow again next spring.

You are very close to the end of the mowing

Re-turfing bald area of lawn

season. Set the blades on the mower high.

The blight of this month and next is fallen leaves. If they're not raked away, they will rot and so will the grass underneath.

FLOWER BEDS & BORDERS

If you think exercise and fresh air will dispel the onset of winter idleness, you can make yourself very busy. Pull up the last of the summer bedding plants and put them on the compost heap, then turn over the ground, digging in a bit of well-rotted compost.

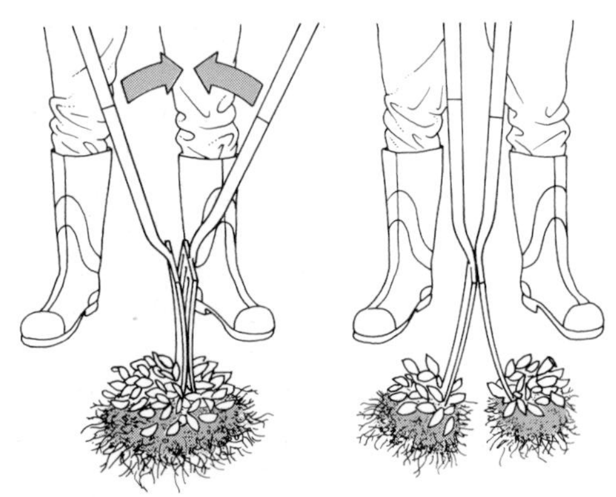

Splitting perennials

Perennials that have grown too big can be lifted and split with two forks, and now is the best time to transplant anything that you think is in the wrong place (see the corresponding section under 'August' for how to do this).

HOUSEPLANTS, WINDOW BOXES, TUBS & TROUGHS

All plants need light, and though your foliage plants are not as demanding as flowering ones, they may like to be a little closer to the window during the winter. As the central heating starts to take command of the atmosphere, so the air gets drier. See page 105 for how to help your houseplants cope with this.

A small environment requires extra management. A mulch on top, and any means of eliminating freezing wind, will help any plant in a tub to survive the winter. Roots of mint and parsley in a pot in the porch, or on the windowsill, will go on growing in winter.

FRUIT TREES & BUSHES

If you do not like chemical sprays, you really should have grease bands round the trunks of your fruit trees. Young trees with smooth bark are easy to treat in this way, but older trees need a bit of putty in the cracks of the bark to ensure a complete barrier to the larvae of that nasty codling moth as they try to crawl upwards. Some gardeners don't really trust the organic method; they spray as well.

If you want another gooseberry or currant bush, prune off a bit of this year's growth, 9in. (22.5cm) or more long, and poke it well down into sandy soil. And if you have no raspberries, visit a neighbour who has. If there are any suckers showing, ask permission, plunge a spade down near the root of the parent plant and you should dig up a stem or two with some roots on them. Plant them in your own garden and invite your neighbour down to the pub.

In preparing to plant any fruit, tree or bush, dig deep, mix in lime and compost, and let it settle for a week or two before planting. If you haven't prepared in advance, the same applies, but pour on more water before and after planting.

WINDOWSILL, COLD FRAME & GREENHOUSE

At this time of year plants are getting desperate for light, so all that shading and dirt on glass or plastic must be washed off.

If you've got heating, and plants that need it, you might consider insulating the greenhouse with plastic. Your garden centre will be awash with advice on how to do it. The difficult calculation is the balance between the cost of insulation and the savings on heating costs. An extra layer of anything reduces light.

You must still ventilate both greenhouse and cold frame every day, but close down at night. Everything under glass should be kept on the dry side.

Keep an eye open for pests: they are persistent, and getting rid of them now is vital.

TREES, SHRUBS & CLIMBERS

All those fallen leaves are potentially valuable compost. If you have mountains of leaves, make a simple wire cage in which to rot them down (see page 74). A spadeful or two of soil well mixed in with them will produce some lovely stuff for next autumn, or use it earlier as a mulch. And don't be proud: no garden produces as much compost as it needs. If you see a big pile of leaves, gather them up.

If you think a small tree or shrub is in the wrong place, transplant it. Dig the hole *before* digging up the plant, as even a few minutes' wait can dry out exposed roots. Get some compost or peat mixed into the soil in the bottom of the hole and try to transfer as much soil around the root as possible. Finally, water, water – even if it is pouring with rain.

GENERAL

It is very easy to lull yourself into a false sense of security: 'The digging can wait until next month; those leaves will blow away; I'll take some cuttings next weekend.' Beware, however – the climate and the gardening season can close down very rapidly.

HOW MUCH HEAT?

To maintain a greenhouse temperature of 45°F (7.2°C) when the outside temperature is only 20°F (−6.6°C) calculate using this formula:

Surface area × 10 = Watts (electric heater)

Surface area × 33 = BTUs (paraffin, gas or oil)

So if your greenhouse has 245 square feet (6.93 square metres) of glass, you would require an electric heater capable of producing 2450 watts, and an oil, paraffin or gas heater capable of producing 8085 BTUs.

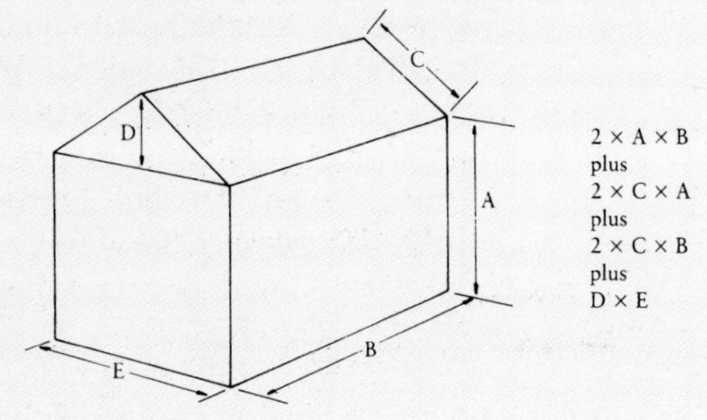

HARDY PLANTS AT BRESSINGHAM

BY ALAN BLOOM

It is no easy matter to strike a balance between growing plants for love and growing them for money. The conflict for me began when I was still in my teens and was not finally resolved until my late forties – a few years after I settled down at Bressingham. At Oakington, near Cambridge, my father grew flowers for market. To cut flowers just as they were coming to their best did not appeal to me and I resolved to produce the plants themselves for sale. This attracted me so much more because, as a nurseryman proper, I could vastly increase the variety of what I grew.

Long before I became established, however, I fell for collecting as many kinds as possible of those plants which appealed to me, with too little regard for demand. But money was far too tight at the time for such an indulgence and I quickly had to make myself concentrate more firmly on making the business commercially viable. So began a phase when necessity steered me on to wholesale production of anything likely to meet a demand. And it led to my 1939 catalogue offering close on 2,000 varieties of perennials and alpines. They occupied 36 acres (14.5 hectares) of land, yet still I hankered for a garden where I could widen the range even more – just for love.

That Bressingham offered full scope for this ambition was one of the reasons for deciding to move there, but first the nursery had to be restored after being decimated by wartime contingencies. There, I believed, I could fulfil all my ambitions – to be nurseryman, gardener and farmer; and so in time, the final balance was achieved.

In the early 1950s, when I had settled at Bressingham, it became obvious that because they were more labour-intensive, perennials and alpines had lost popularity in favour of shrubs and ground-coverers. With no desire to follow the trend, it was up to me to do all in my power to restore perennials and alpines to favour, for I believed that they offer unique value in garden worthiness if used and grown sensibly. This became a mission, and apart from writing articles in the gardening papers and books, it led to the formation of the Hardy Plant Society and the development of a large garden composed of island beds in which plants could flourish with the minimum of after care.

At last my latent collecting urge was allowed full vent. But the cri-

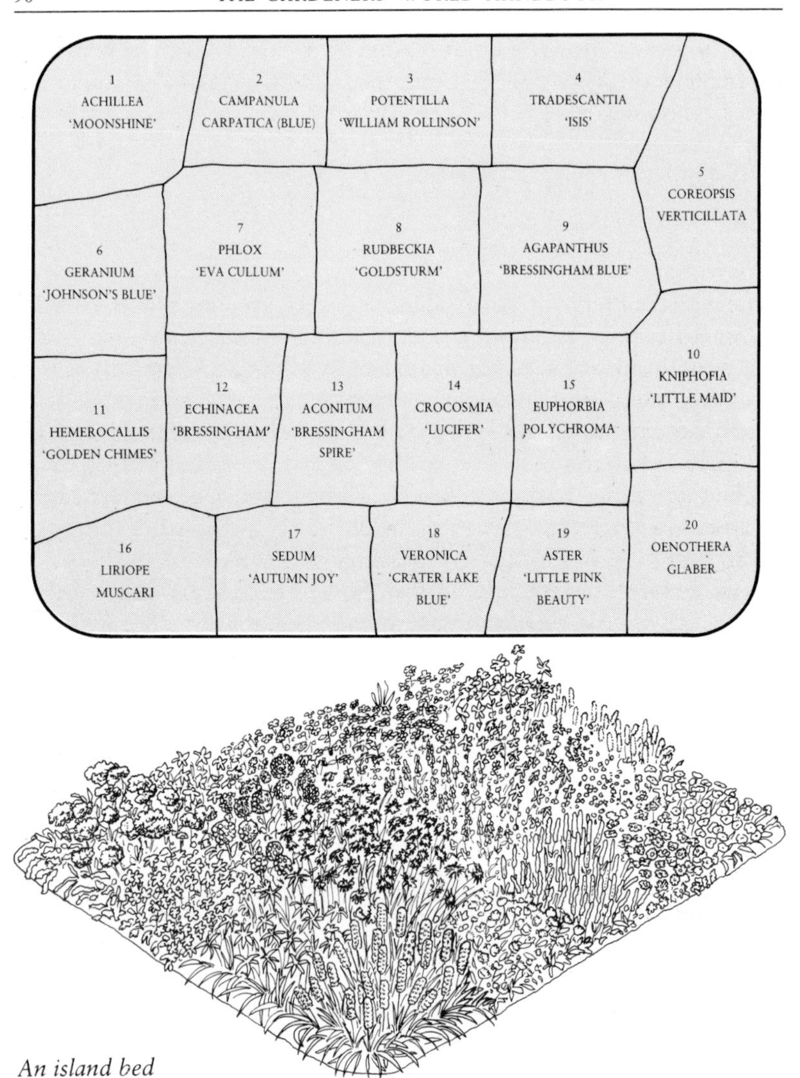

An island bed

terion which guided me was always that of garden worthiness. As new arrivals came – often as a result of swapping specimens with botanic and private gardens in Britain and abroad – each was assessed on its merits. In cases where I obtained only a single plant or some seed or cuttings, several years might pass before I could formulate a judgement – and often the best means of propagation was discovered by trial and error. Not all I acquired flourished where first placed, and further trials were sometimes needed. Such factors as shade, soil and moisture requirements had also to be discovered – and not all were finally met.

The necessary attributes and qualifications for garden worthiness are simple enough. A subject should be reliably hardy and perennial, whether classed as a border plant or alpine; it should have either flower or foliage appeal, and preferably both; it should not be excessively tall and ungainly, thus needing supports, and should not be invasive. Our cross between the invasive antholyza and *Crocosmia masonorum* yielded the spectacular varieties 'Lucifer' and 'Firebird', which are virtually without fault.

The matter of adaptability is important, but a species should not be downgraded if it will flourish only in narrow environmental limits – in acid, moist or peaty soil, for example, or in shade; or, at the other extreme, in dry, stony, limy soil in full sun.

The majority of perennials prefer sun to shade, and although abundant information is available for those about to make a selection, one may find, as I have, that some plants are more adaptable than advisory literature has indicated.

Only a minority of perennials have to be given special treatment. Generally this is to provide as closely as possible the conditions of the subject's native habitat. Sometimes a wrong climate is the cause of failure, but those to whom choice or difficult plants appeal should not be deterred by this because micro climates can be created. I managed to succeed with the charming little blue *Corydalis cashmeriana*, but it took me a few years before it finally settled happily in a north-facing peat bed. As a nurseryman I find that such treasures come as a challenge, but the incentive goes well beyond the profit motive.

The exquisite double white *Trillium grandiflorum* is another example worth mentioning. In 1958 nine plants arrived from Montreal Botanic Garden with the advice that they grew best in heavy soil and in shade. After three years, however, they were divided to make only twos and threes each, and only after ten years had increased to a hundred. Stubbornly I refused high prices offered by those who wanted to buy them. Instead I began experimenting with means of more rapid increase and with different soils, adding more and more humus along with sharp sand. It worked, and although it still takes five years to produce a flowering-size plant, I am at last able to release a hundred or so annually for sale, and still show an increase in the back-up stock.

This is an extreme example of how necessary it is to be adaptable and adopt a rational attitude where stocks of choice, rare or new plants are concerned. In contrast to the trillium, a new Michaelmas daisy selected as a seedling worth naming and introducing can be increased to a thousand plants for sale after two years. Most of the hundred or so subjects I have raised and introduced over the past fifty-five years have been increased by division or cuttings to upwards of a thousand plants for sale over a period of from three to ten years. This period includes the whittling-down process which may be spread over three years when perhaps twenty or more first selections from a large batch are finally reduced to a few, or even only one, worth naming and introducing.

Stock control is a vital factor in production. It affects both quantity and quality. One has to plan ahead, sometimes years ahead, in order to have reserves for future sales. Only the commoner perennials and alpines can be produced by an annual routine from seed, to become of saleable quality within a year.

Where the means of increase is by division or cuttings, reserve stocks must be available at the correct time as propagating material. One learns the best means of propagating from hard-won experience, and timing can make all the difference between success and failure. Mishaps can so easily occur, as I found when two of my quite outstanding pyrethrums were killed off by someone's lack of care with weed-killer just as stocks were within a year of launching. I'd named them 'Venus' and 'Inferno' in anticipation.

One also has to be firm and refuse orders which would deplete reserve stocks, and calculations of future requirements based on expected demand have to be quite meticulous. Sale catalogues have to be compiled months ahead of distribution, so the task of projecting both the demand and the supply is as vital as it is difficult.

It follows, of course, that the greater the variety of plants one grows and offers for sale, the more difficult stock control becomes. If one includes, as we now do, conifers, heathers and shrubs, one has to departmentalise under separate managers and production schedules and facilities. In my retirement from involvement in the day-to-day running of the nursery, I manage a mere 500 or so kinds of perennials on 5 acres (2 hectares) of nursery near my house, to work up stocks of new introductions.

My helpers and I, apart from this and caring for the 5-acre (2-hectare) display garden, look after trials. These are of such subjects as hostas, paeonias, irises and hemerocallis, which have proliferous varieties needing to be tried out in order to select the best. The display garden plays its part in the complex as a trial ground for the worthiness of many other new acquisitions. It also yields seed requirements as well as cuttings and dividable stock to meet the nursery shortages.

What I look upon as my nursery is not mechanised as is the rest of Bressingham. We plant and pot by hand and are in general old-fashioned in our methods, but losses are minimised thereby, and amongst the variety we grow are many choice and treasured kinds.

The arrival of plastic pots, along with an increasingly mobile population, has brought about the proliferation of garden centres. These in turn have made more people garden-conscious. The result has been a much greater emphasis on cash-and-carry sales of nursery produce.

Costs of production have soared and people are willing to pay more for what they buy, often on impulse, on seeing well-presented containerised stock. Yet these same plants can be obtained at little more than half the cost by those who are willing to wait for bare-root-grown stock in autumn or spring.

Some plant offers are advertised in the press at what might appear to be ridiculously low prices by firms who are merely traders. What most of them do is to contract with a grower for large quantities of a very limited, easily produced range. Price rather than quality is the governing factor, and the Dutchmen are experts at this. When comparisons are made in size and quality with well-grown flowering-sized stock, these seemingly cheap offers are in fact the more expensive. In no other field of production and sales can there be so great a diversity in quality and price, and some gardeners gullibly go for the cheapest.

Some garden centres are, of course, out to compete on price with little regard for quality. But at least people can see what they are buying, whereas those who fall for cheap mail order offers cannot do so. Few garden centres have staff capable of advising customers, but those who have knowledgeable sales people, along with those who display a wide variety of well-grown stock, are likely to be the most successful in the long run. The long-running television programmes such as *Gardeners' World* are proof not only of the widespread interest in gardening, but also of the need for sound advice on the many facets of cultivation and the vast range of the wonderful world of plants.

For thirty years I resisted supplying other than the trade in the hope that our wholesale customers would supply what we grew to the gardening public. However, so few were interested in the less common kinds of plants that we had to embark on retail sales as well. Only by this means could growing a wide variety be justified on economic grounds. Since then the retail section has grown enormously, but so has the basic wholesale side. What I should have perceived long ago is that some retailing is a vital factor in supporting my constant urge to collect or breed and select the widest possible range of garden-worthy plants, and I should have offered sooner to share them at a reasonable price with the now ever-growing band of people interested in hardy perennials.

My hopes for the future are still lively – just as *Achillea* 'Moonshine', which I all but discarded for lack of thorough trial, and which is now a firm favourite in thousands of gardens. Perhaps two new astilbes, 'Rosemary Bloom' and 'Elizabeth Bloom', and 'Anthea', another new achillea, all now in intensive production, will be equally popular in a few years' time.

A SEED IN TIME

BY ROY LANCASTER

Growing into an old thorn tree on my garden boundary is a climbing rose from China. I planted it as a seedling four years ago and it is already some 20ft (6m) high, its branches threading their way into a neighbouring birch. It has not flowered yet and until it does I cannot be sure of its identity, though I have my suspicions. The seed from which it grew came from one of a handful of hips picked from a plant growing in a thicket on an exposed hillside in the Chinese province of Sichuan close to the border with Tibet. With luck, it will flower next year at seven years of age, and then I can look forward to an annual cascade of white sweetly fragrant blossoms.

Not all the plants I have grown from seed collected in the wild have taken as long to reach flowering maturity. A fiery red campion, *Lychnis fulgens*, also from China, was flowering in its first year, as was a colourful clarkia from California – but then, clarkias are annuals and one naturally expects quick results from them. Although it is not uncommon for one's seedlings to flower earlier than expected, it is more usual to have to wait several years for the event. In a funny way, the longer seedlings take to flower, the greater the excitement and pleasure when they finally make it. I have been collecting and growing plants from seed for twenty years or more and not a year goes by without one or other of my seedlings flowering for the first time.

This year it was a rock lily (*Arthropodium cirrhatum*) collected from a sheltered sea cliff in the Bay of Islands, New Zealand, in 1985. This is a tender plant outside in our climate but one of the seedlings I raised I potted on to grow in our home and now it has rewarded us with a charming display of white star-shaped flowers. The seed of the rock lily is small, abundant and easily germinated, and from only a handful of capsules I found myself with hundreds of seedlings, most of which I gave away to friends and neighbours.

Sometimes seed is not only in short supply but all kinds of potential disasters attend its germination. In 1980 I collected just six seeds of a golden pomegranate in Peking. Despite great care, two of the seeds went missing in transit. Of the remaining four, two I gave to a nurseryman friend and two I sowed myself. My friend's seed refused to germinate, presumably because it was not viable, while my seed produced seedlings. Unfortunately, one of these subsequently died from causes unknown while the other I pampered in a pot in a cold greenhouse.

Two years later this seedling, having grown into a small bush 12in. (30cm) high, began to look unhappy so, taking the bull by the horns, I planted it in a narrow border at the foot of the south-facing wall of our house. Thankfully, it has settled down and at the time of writing is 4ft (1.2m) tall and flourishing. It has not flowered yet, and it will be several years before I know if it has golden fruits like the mother plant, but even if the fruits are red, it will have been well worth the wait.

Since it became illegal to dig up wild plants on holidays abroad more and more gardeners have taken to collecting seed as a source of living souvenirs and it really does make better sense. Not only is seed small, light and convenient to carry compared with plants, but there is also less likelihood of pests and diseases being inadvertently brought into the home country. Some seeds are so small that a mere pinch can provide enough plants to satisfy one's own needs with sufficient spares to please all one's friends as well as the local WI market and church fete. A single rose hip, for instance, contains upwards of two dozen seeds, while a poppy capsule contains hundreds if not thousands.

Growing plants from seed has its surprises too. The seed of an unknown but potentially new hydrangea in my garden was received from China as a spiraea! And a silky seed head given me as that of a clematis turned out to be a pasque flower (*Pulsatilla*). My prize for the strangest plant source, however, goes to the anonymous sender of a packet labelled 'seed from a toffee apple eaten in Kunming'. One result of this curious present is a 6ft (1.8m) tree in my garden which looks to be more of a Chinese hawthorn (*Crataegus*) than an apple. I can hardly wait for it to flower and fruit.

Yet collecting seed is only an exciting preliminary to the serious business of growing it. Different seeds have different requirements for germination, and although the subject has attracted a whole catalogue of books and articles, some of them detailed and technical, there are one or two basic 'rules of thumb' which, if observed, will bring reasonable success to beginners. Every gardener knows, or should know, that seeds need moisture, oxygen and warmth to germinate, to which light must be added once germination has taken place. Comparatively few seeds will germinate and grow in permanently wet conditions; so a seed compost should be open and well drained to allow excess water to escape and to facilitate the free movement of air (oxygen).

Generally speaking, large, fleshy, firm-coated seeds like oak, chestnut, maple, camellia and so on quickly dehydrate if left lying around and will refuse to germinate. These seeds are best sown as soon as they are ripe – preferably when recently fallen from the plant. They can be sown to a depth equal to their own size singly in pots or, if a larger quantity is involved, broadcast or spaced along a drill drawn in a prepared bed in the garden. Such seeds will germinate the following year or, in the case of oak, often the same year. Be sure, however, to protect these seeds from the attentions of mice and squirrels. A simple method involves the use of chicken wire to cover the pot or drill.

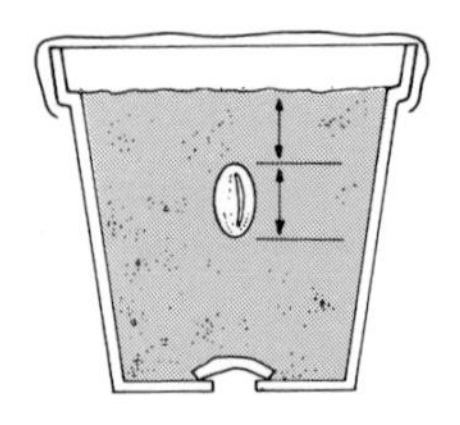

Sowing a large, firm-coated seed

Smaller fleshy-coated seeds (fruits, more correctly) like those of berberis, cotoneaster, viburnum, dogwood, mountain ash and roses can be stratified – that is, sown between layers of coarse grit in a pot or box and placed outside to receive a winter freezing – after which they can be sown in the normal way in February or March. Germination usually takes place a year later. There are, as a matter of interest, a large number of plants whose seeds need some degree of cold treatment in order to germinate. As an alternative to stratification, more and more gardeners are storing such seeds in damp sand or peat in a polythene bag then placing them in the fridge (but not the freezer) for several weeks before sowing in the normal way in February.

By far the majority of seed types one collects, though, are relatively small and more easily stored in cool, dry, frost-free conditions. Many of our most popular and attractive garden flowers are found in this category: poppy, mallow, rock rose, spiraea, mock orange, campanula, hosta and geranium are just a few examples. Although these can be sown on ripening, I have always had better results from sowing them under glass (no heat required) in February or March. A cold frame is equally useful and so long as the compost is not allowed to dry out the seed should germinate within weeks. Freshly sown seed need not be kept in the dark in order to germinate, but it must not be exposed to direct sunlight, especially under glass, as this will inhibit germination and desiccate fragile newly germinated seedlings.

Of course, there are many exceptions to the above, nor will books and professional advice provide all the answers. Trial and error will always feature in one's efforts, especially when dealing with unusual or unfamiliar seeds; but then, that is all part of the attraction. If every seed germinated as easily as mustard and cress we would have no challenges and nothing to replace the annual satisfaction of another success.

HOUSEPLANTS

BY ANNE SWITHINBANK

There must be few houses around the country which have no houseplants at all. I cannot imagine living in a home without the softening effect of leaves and shoots and the occasional bright exotic effect of flowers.

However, keeping houseplants healthy is not always an easy matter. Good subjects for beginners are *Rhoicissus rhomboidea* (grape ivy), aspidistra, palms, tradescantia (wandering Jew), cordyline, chlorophytum (spider plant), two types of ficus (rubber plant, weeping fig) and monstera (Swiss cheese plant). Once the art of growing these has been mastered, there is a vast range of plants available.

There are many books to tell us how to care for houseplants. I would prefer to approach the problem of looking after them by first considering what they *don't* like.

WHY DO HOUSEPLANTS DIE?

Winter

Winter is by far the biggest killer of houseplants. Central heating dries out the air, and this is not tolerated by most plants. It causes unsightly browning of the tips and edges of the leaves, which then dry out completely and eventually drop off. In the wild many of our common houseplants live in very humid places. Plants are constantly losing moisture through their leaves, so it is easy to understand that for many plants with a tropical origin the centrally heated living room is a very hostile

Grouping plants in a gravel tray

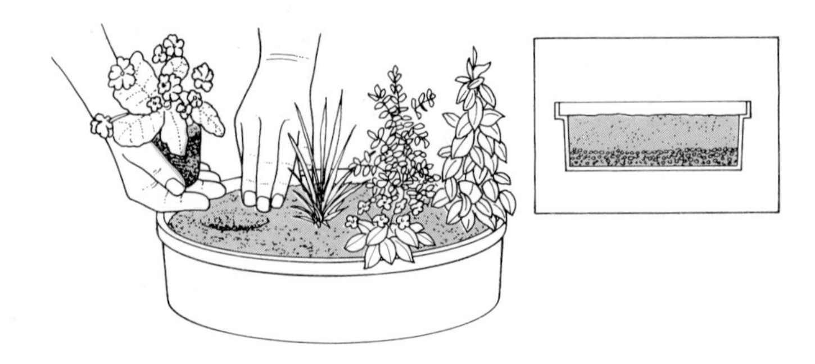

Planting several plants in a large dish, using expanded clay particles or gravel for drainage

place. Instead of leaving a plant to take its chance, I like to help it as much as possible by increasing the moisture in the air about it. This can be done in several ways.

Grouping plants together is very good for them. I have six or seven large specimens standing together. They all benefit from the moisture given off by each other and evaporation from the soil in the pots.

Try using a gravel tray. This is a large container with water in the bottom and enough gravel so that when the plant pot is stood on top, it does not stand in the water. Moisture will then evaporate around it.

Plant several plants together in an attractive large dish or small tub. I have a pottery bowl which I found at a jumble sale. It has no drainage hole, but I solved this problem putting a layer of expanded clay particles (gravel could be used instead) in the bottom. Any excess water drains into this layer instead of clogging up the compost. Using a peat-based compost I have planted *Dieffenbachia picta* (dumb cane), *Adiantum capillus-veneris* (maidenhair fern) and *Scirpus cernuus* (trailing bulrush), which all like humidity and benefit from the moisture given off by each other and by the soil around them. I am sure that I would have a great deal of trouble keeping them alive if they were planted in individual pots, especially the maidenhair fern.

Some plant keepers manage to increase the humidity around their plants by misting them with a fine spray. This must be done with water at room temperature. I find this method impractical, however, as it has to be done in the kitchen or you end up with very damp walls.

Central heating is also responsible for fluctuations in temperature, and the same plants which dislike dry air are also susceptible to these. So many people describe their plants to me as looking very sad with yellowing leaves which drop off, and these are all likely to be victims of extreme temperature variation. Varieties particularly affected are dieffenbachia, croton, caladium, anthurium (flamingo flower), *Beloperone guttata* (shrimp plant) and poinsettia. Plants would rather adapt to a lower but constant temperature if possible. Certainly keep all plants except those which need maximum winter light away from windows where they may suffer cold draughts, and never leave a plant on a windowsill behind closed curtains in winter for the temperature can plummet drastically in such a situation.

Lack of light in winter may not kill plants but it can severely affect their growth. I am lucky enough to have some good south-facing windows which receive maximum winter light. Plants which really need to keep growing during winter are kept near these windows. I encourage other plants, including bougainvillea, to become dormant by giving them much less water than usual and moving them to a cool spare room. Most foliage houseplants, however, just need to be kept going. They will not grow a lot, so feeding can be reduced. I stop liquid feeding altogether and give a slow-release fertiliser only to plants which continue to grow or are building up to flower. Definitely avoid high-nitrogen feeds during winter because these promote leafy growth, which without good light would be very weak and straggly.

Winter light is also a problem for those plants which are building themselves up to flower during this time, such as stephanotis, *Jasminum polyanthum*, cymbidium, citrus and desert cacti which require as much light as possible from a south-facing window. Other plants need short days to flower. Only when they are reduced to a certain number of hours of light will they produce flower buds instead of leafy shoots. These plants include *Schlumbergera truncata* (Christmas cactus) and poinsettia. So many owners of Christmas cacti complain that their plants, although very healthy, never flower. They do not realise that because the plants are kept in their living room they are receiving artificial light during winter evenings. This will prevent them from developing flower buds. Giving your Christmas cactus a nice warm fireside place next to the television will not guarantee a profusion of flowers in return.

A poinsettia will produce red bracts during natural winter light. However, if it receives any unnatural light at all it will not respond in the same way. If necessary you will have to cover the plant with black plastic or similar blackout material. It should have no less than fourteen hours of darkness each day for eight weeks, usually from about mid-September onwards.

Both buying plants and bringing them home during winter are potentially lethal operatons. My advice is not to buy any at all until late spring – apart from seasonal plants to brighten up the winter months.

If you have been saving up for a really big expensive plant to fill a corner, remember that it will settle into the house much better during the warmer part of the year. The problem is that even if plants have been kept in ideal conditions before you buy them, they have got to adjust to room conditions at home. If they have spent even a short time in a draughty shop with the door opening and closing, or worse still outside the shop, they may even be dying when you buy them.

Physically getting a plant home in cold weather is hazardous. If a few leaves are poking out of a shopping bag and the temperature is anywhere around zero, it will probably die. A friend of mine left three assorted houseplants in the back of her car one winter night and three days later they were black and frosted.

Overwatering

Overwatering must surely be one of the biggest killers of houseplants. When asked 'How often should I water?' I always wish I could answer with precise infallible instructions. Unfortunately it is not as easy as that, but then it is not so difficult either.

Imagine the plant roots growing in the soil. They need to breathe as much as the rest of the plant. If you keep all the small air spaces in the soil constantly filled with water, the roots will suffocate, stop taking up water and the plant, denied this, will wilt and die. The only sure way to discover whether or not a plant needs watering is to look at or feel the surface of the compost. In most cases the correct time to water is when the surface has begun to dry out and become crumbly, but well before the whole pot is dry, which would result in the plant wilting.

Having decided that a plant is dry, water it liberally from the top. Should any water remain in the saucer, empty it out. Avoid very small, frequent applications of water. Many houseplant growers are under the impression that it is good practice to water from the bottom by filling up the saucer. I have never used this method with my plants. However, although I do not recommend it, I would say that if you are used to this method and it works, continue to use it.

This guide to watering applies to most houseplants. As with other aspects of care it pays to imagine where the plants might be growing in the wild. Pelargoniums, cacti and succulents can withstand and benefit from drying out almost completely between waterings as they would normally have to cope with this. Ferns and azaleas, however, dislike becoming too dry. In their case even the surface of the compost should not become too dry. Provided the compost is not so wet that water could be squeezed out of it, they can be watered. Some plants, such as cyperus (umbrella plant), enjoy boggy conditions and can be left standing in water continuously, although this is not necessary.

If a plant is overwatered, the first thing to do is wait until the compost has dried out again. It should be as dry as you dare let it become before the next watering. Changing the compost in such a case, in my experience, usually results in the plant dying. This is because the few remaining live roots are ripped away. If the plant seems to take ages to dry out, this can be speeded up. Knock the plant out of its pot and, without disturbing the roots, stand the rootball on top of the inverted pot in a dry place. Keep a close eye on the process so that you don't allow it to become too dry.

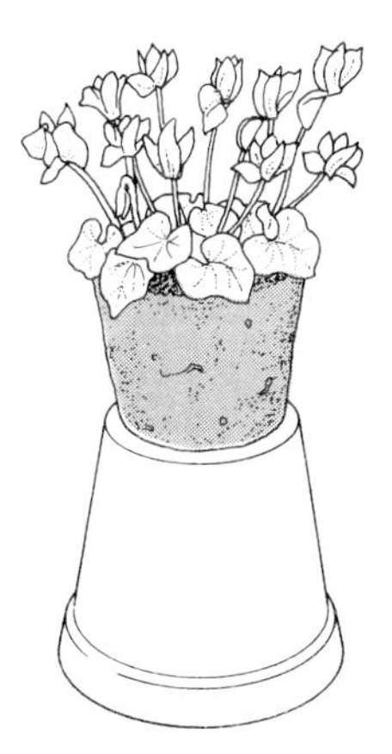

Drying out an overwatered plant

Underwatering

Plants can tolerate a certain amount of underwatering, although if this occurs regularly their health will be affected. Growth will be stunted and flower buds drop off. If, however great your efforts, you do not find time to inspect your plants regularly for watering, you could try plunging the plant pot in a larger container of moist peat.

I have seen plants underwatered by being given a little dribble of water regularly, usually by owners scared stiff of overwatering. When I decide that a plant needs watering, I always give it a good soak, and then wait until it has dried out again sufficiently for another one. In this way all the roots receive water and not just the top few inches.

Killing With Kindness

I am quite sure that some houseplant owners have killed their plants by paying them too much attention. We have dealt with overwatering, but overfeeding can also be harmful. When a plant has become established in the potting compost (usually after six weeks to two months in the growing season), it should be given fertiliser. This can be applied in one of several ways.

The most usual is a liquid feed added to the water – follow the instructions given with the product. Never feed a dry plant. If necessary, water first and feed a little later. As a general guide most houseplants should be fed every two weeks during spring, summer and autumn.

If, like me, you are very busy and find it hard to remember to feed the plants, use a slow-release fertiliser which can be applied and forgotten about, usually for about two months at a time.

Should you have a plant which is looking very starved, the quickest way to get the feed in is to apply it as a foliar spray.

It is useful to know the content of fertilisers. Quoted on the bottle or packet somewhere should be the ratio of N:P:K (nitrogen: phosphorus: potassium). Most foliage houseplants prefer a high N feed, which encourages leafy growth. Should you want a plant to flower or fruit, a high K fertiliser (like tomato fertiliser) will help this. Otherwise the elements should be well balanced. During winter I do not like to continue giving my plants a high N fertiliser. As light is low, any leafy growth they make is liable to be spindly. I prefer them to build themselves up and start growing profusely again in spring. I usually give a slow-release feed of equal parts N, P and K during winter. Remember that giving plants too much feed at any time of year can be harmful.

Sprays to control pests and diseases can also damage plants if they are applied in concentrations above those recommended in the manufacturer's instructions. Always read chemical instructions fully. This is important for the health of you, the family and pets as well as the plant. 'Spray damage' on houseplants appears as scorch marks or distortions of the leaves and growing points.

I have seen houseplants damaged by over assiduous cleaning. It is important to keep the leaf surfaces free of dust and dirt so that they can continue to absorb light, which they need for growth. Dusting lightly will remove most dirt from leaves. With large strong leaves I carefully use the brush attachment on the vacuum cleaner. Hairy leaves can be cleaned very effectively with a small paintbrush. I have an aversion to the leaf cleaning 'preparations' available. They will harm some leaves and cannot be used on hairy or young leaves. They are most often used on large, smooth, thick leaves, like those of the rubber plant, to shine them up. I prefer the leaves to look natural.

WHAT IS FOLIAR FEEDING?

All plants can take up food through openings (stomata) in their leaves and thence into the sap stream. Foliar feeding is a particularly useful treatment when applied to sickly plants with poor root growth, and is beneficial for houseplants.

HOW TO COPE WITH THE 'FEW LEAVES ON TOP OF A LONG STEM' SYNDROME

This problem is common in monstera (Swiss cheese plant), ficus, fatshedera, beloperone (shrimp plant), yucca and aphelandra (zebra plant).

It happens to the best of us and is usually the result of the plant getting old. I generally set about rejuvenation by taking cuttings or air-layering the top of the plant, followed by cutting the main stem right down almost to the bottom, always cutting above a node (the slight swelling round the stem where leaves used to be). Around the node area and on nodes below, there should be potential buds, which will then grow to make a new plant.

Always remember that when a plant has been cut down it needs a position of good light to encourage new growth. It should not be potted on, or fed, until the new growths have appeared and started to grow strongly.

Going back to the top part of the plant, this is where the cuttings will be taken from. They will be of soft or semi-hard wood, which is really anything but obviously old thick barky stem. Make a clean cut below a node about 3in. (7.5cm) from the tip of a small shoot – further if it is a large plant like a monstera or ficus. Trim the lower leaves from the cutting, dip into hormone rooting powder and dibble it into a mixture of equal parts of peat and sharp grit. Cuttings need reasonable light in which to root. However, direct scorching sun will dry them up too much. A propagating case, or a plastic cover or even a plastic bag placed over their pot and kept off the cuttings with canes, will help them to root. It is a good idea to allow a little air in.

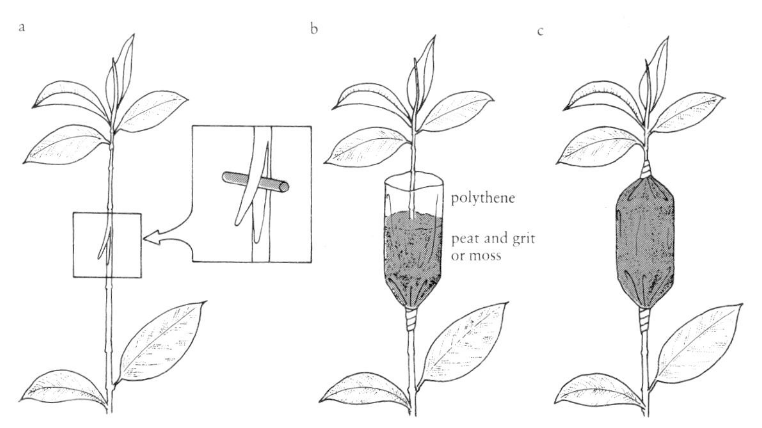

a *Wedge the cut open with a twig*
b *Wrap polythene round the stem, then fill with peat and grit or moss*
c *Tie polythene firmly at the top*

Air-layering is an excellent method of propagating plants such as rubber plants, especially if you have no place to root cuttings. The idea is to get the plant to produce roots before you take the 'cutting' off. Select a portion of fairly young stem about 15in. (38cm) from the top of the plant. Make a slanting cut upwards, beginning ¾in. (2cm) below a node so that the top of the cut is about half-way into the stem (no more) at the position of the node. (Remember that a node is the point on the stem where the leaves come out. If the node you want to cut up to has a leaf, simply remove that leaf.) Wedge the cut with some moss or a sliver of wood. Make a sleeve of black plastic around the area of the cut. Tie it below the cut, removing more leaves if necessary. Fill the 'bag' with a mixture of moist peat and grit or wrap the stem in sphagnum moss. Make it firm around the cut. Tie the end of the sleeve tightly above the cut. In six weeks to two months, roots should have grown out and you should be able to feel them through the plastic. Cut off the rooted portion of the plant and pot it up into a good potting compost.

Shrimp plants often become leggy when they have flowered for a long time. All the shoots can be trimmed down to within one or two nodes of the base. Softwood cuttings about 3in. (7.5cm) long can then be made from the trimmings – if any flowers remain, simply nip them off. I usually fit six or seven cuttings into a 3½in. (9cm) pot.

Always remember that cuttings, air-layering or any unusual activity to do with houseplants should take place between April and September while the plants are active. Only in emergencies should propagation be attempted during the dark months of winter.

MAKING MORE PLANTS

Propagation is great fun and very rewarding. It is also quite possible to increase houseplants without greenhouses and expensive equipment.

Pots full of ordinary shoot cuttings can be rooted in polythene bags, as has already been explained. A north-facing windowsill is an ideal position for these.

Many cuttings root quite happily in water. I think it is worth trying almost any cutting to see if it will work. At Kew Gardens they have a beautiful plant called the jade vine, and for years they could not persuade it to root. One day they left some shoots in a bucket of water in the corner of a shed and forgot about them. Several weeks later somebody was cleaning out the shed when they found the bucket and discovered that the cuttings had rooted in the water. Other less exotic plants that will do this are tradescantia, impatiens (busy Lizzie), cyperus (umbrella plant) and saintpaulia (African violet) leaf cuttings. A useful tip is to put a piece of aluminium foil over the top of the water

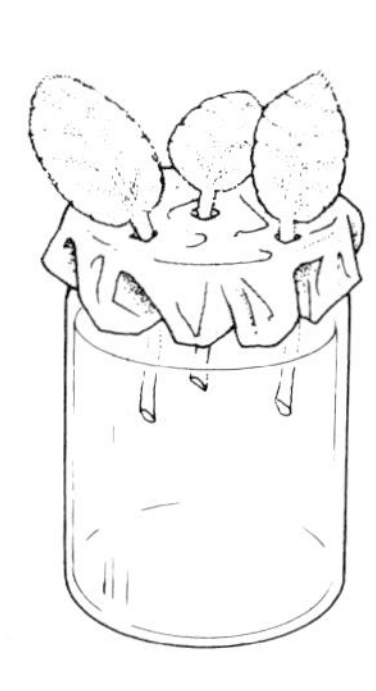

Propagating from leaf cuttings and an avocado stone

jar and poke the stems of the cuttings through this so that the bottom 1in. (2.5cm) or so of each is in the water.

Plants that produce offsets are great fun and easy to propagate in the house. *Tolmiea menziesii* (piggy back plant), *Saxifraga stolonifera* (mother of thousands), *Asplenium bulbiferum* (a beautiful easy-to-grow fern) and, of course, the well-known chlorophytum (spider plant) are examples of these. Simply detach the offsets and push them into some potting compost in a small pot. Water them in and they should quickly develop their own roots and grow. Failing this, place small pots of compost around the mother plant, stick the babies in while still attached and only separate them when they have got going.

Growing plants from seed can be very successful indoors. Good easy seeds to start with are citrus 'pips', which are best sown as soon as they are taken out of the fruit. Use seed compost and just push them into the surface so that they are covered by their own width with compost. Keeping the compost moist is very important. I sowed some kumquat pips in February and covered the pot with clingfilm. I placed it in the airing cupboard, and within two weeks the seeds were germinating. It is important to remove the pot to a light window as soon as the seedlings appear, and take off the clingfilm to give them room to develop.

During summer it is not necessary to use the airing cupboard, and many different types of pips can be tried. Avocado stones can be balanced over water by pushing four cocktail sticks around the neck of the stone. Sometimes avocados take months to germinate, at other times only a week or two.

Seeds of houseplants can be bought from seed firms and germinated according to the instructions on the packet. Remember to keep them moist and at the correct temperature for germination. Give them as much light as possible to encourage growth without scorching them.

FIVE FAVOURITES

I think the following make excellent houseplants.

Stephanotis

This is expensive to buy, but I love it for its glossy green foliage and beautiful white scented flowers. When you buy a stephanotis, it is usually in flower. This has almost certainly been forced by strictly controlled high temperatures and lighting. The first important thing is to try to give the plant as even a temperature as possible when you get it home, and plenty of light. (Mine lives 3ft (90cm) away from a big south-facing window.) This is very important for subsequent flowering. Under ordinary room conditions flowering usually starts about May, but it is wholly dependent on the quality of light and temperature received in winter. My own plant withstood temperature fluctuations of between about 55° and 70°F (13° and 21°C). A word of warning: fix your stephanotis up with a good climbing frame. Re-potting, if required, can be done either in early spring or later in the summer.

Begonia masoniana (Iron Cross begonia)

An excellent foliage begonia with very striking markings in the shape of the Iron Cross, this plant tolerates room conditions well. It prefers to become quite dry on the surface of the compost between watering.

Gesneria macrantha

Bright red heads of tubular flowers 2–3in. (5–7.5cm) long are produced almost continuously by this plant. If it becomes tatty, it can be dried off to a tuber and started off again after a rest. Seed sown in March will give flowering plants by the end of the summer.

Brunfelsia calycina 'Macrantha'

This is a very beautiful shrubby plant with blue flowers 3in. (7.5cm) across. Because these turn different shades of blue as they open and fade, it goes by the common name of 'yesterday, today and tomorrow plant'. It can tolerate quite low temperatures, although it will drop a few leaves if exposed to draughts. My specimen has been living by a north-facing glass door and occasionally gets a draught from the cat door. However, it has rewarded me with an abundance of flowers. It starts flowering in April and continues on and off throughout the summer. It benefited from a slow-release feed applied in winter.

Aspidistra elatior 'Variegata'

I am very fond of all aspidistras, but it is worth looking around for the variegated form. It will show much better variegation in good light, but will still survive in very dark corners. This is really why I like these plants so much. I have lived in several houses with appalling light for houseplants, and I have not forgotten the old faithfuls which continued to survive under these conditions. Aspidistras are tough. To an extent they can tolerate dry air, cold temperatures and some draughts.

WINTER

NOVEMBER
DECEMBER
JANUARY

STORING VEGETABLES AND FRUIT
Clay Jones

PAVING AND WALLS
Geoff Hamilton

GARDEN VISITING
Ashley Stephenson

NOVEMBER

VEGETABLE PATCH

Dirty days hath November – and the best excuse of all for not toiling away at anything is that working or walking on waterlogged soil does more harm than good. However, there will be fine days, and the digging beckons. Throw some lime about as you dig, except where you plan to put next year's early potatoes.

You can plant broad beans in a sheltered spot, and horseradish.

You should have some globe artichokes, possibly in the flower border. Wherever they are, chop them right down and put 4 or 5in. (10 or 12.5cm) of compost on top of the roots to protect them from frost. It is infuriating, particularly if you've grown them from seed, to lose them in the first winter.

If you are a tidy gardener, there will be no diseased-looking refuse lying about. If you're not, clean it up, but *don't* put it on the compost heap. Burn it if you can, if not put it in the dustbin.

Put an upturned box over the rhubarb.

LAWN

Delight in the knowledge that doing nothing at all is best.

FLOWER BEDS & BORDERS

A very thorough clean-up really is important. All the decaying or diseased-looking bits of everything from roses and herbaceous perennials need to be removed. Decayed material

HOW MUCH LINER FOR A POOL?

Measure the pool at its widest and longest points and add twice the planned depth to both the length and width. So if the pool is 10ft (3m) long and 5ft (1.5m) wide and is to be 3ft (1m) deep, you will require a sheet of liner 10ft + 6ft = 16ft (3m + 1.8m = 4.8m) long by 5ft + 6ft = 11ft (1.5m + 1.8m = 3.3m) wide. The liner will need to be 16ft by 11ft (4.8m by 3.3m).

must go to the compost heap; diseased should be burnt or dustbinned.

Don't get over-enthusiastic, though. Leave everything that is green and healthy; that's still providing food for the plants. The dead but not decayed may provide winter protection, a sort of natural mulch, so leave that alone too.

Anything that sticks up high will be pushed about by the wind and should be shortened. Rocking loosens the roots and lets water in, and flooded roots freeze very quickly.

Frost will lift the soil round young plants, so put a boot about them. If you are passing the garden centre, go in and buy some bargain spring-flowering bulbs: they will be clearing their shelves now. Plant these deeply on a bit of sand if it is very wet.

HOUSEPLANTS, WINDOW BOXES TUBS & TROUGHS

Light and not too much water are the prerequisites of houseplants, and those rooted cuttings must be looked after like babies.

If they are not too heavy, move tubs and troughs to a sheltered sunny position.

FRUIT TREES & BUSHES

This is a good time to plant new fruit trees and bushes, but stake well to prevent wind wiggle loosening the roots.

Fertilise with phosphate and potash, spread at 4oz to the square yard (125g to the square metre) over the root area, and rake it in. Your garden centre should stock it. Don't waste money on nitrogen at this time of year; indeed, avoid it.

WINDOWSILL, COLD FRAME & GREENHOUSE

Sow some mustard and cress: it will cheer you up watching it grow, and it is good to eat in salads and sandwiches.

The rug over the cold frame and keeping the greenhouse warm become a perpetual responsibility at this point, so watch the weather forecast. Don't forget to ventilate when it is fine.

HOW MANY FISH?

The rule of thumb is 2in. (5cm) of fish for each square foot (900 square centimetres) of pool. So in 20 square feet (1.8 square metres) you can have 20 × 2in. (5cm) fish, 10 × 4in. (10cm) fish, or 5 × 8in. (20cm) fish. Do not put the fish in until next year and remember not to overstock the pool.

TREES, SHRUBS & CLIMBERS

Now is a good time to plant new trees, shrubs and climbers. Be careful not to put wall plants where they will grow up to cover air bricks, and consider too how you are going to fix them to the wall. It's not a bad idea to drill a few holes, bang in rawlplugs and screw in brass hooks.

When planting, plenty of compost and a generous handful of bonemeal mixed with the soil at the bottom of the hole, at least a bucket of water applied as soon as the new plant is in, and then a thick mulch of peat or compost placed around the plant, will assure success (or, to be more truthful, ensure that the plant has a good chance of survival).

Any bare-rooted plants that you buy need to be planted immediately, unless the ground is frozen. If it is too wet to put them in their proper place, dig a trench, stuff them in, and firm down well with a heavy boot.

GENERAL

November is usually a pretty foul month without much excitement. Dig a couple of parnsips and roast them. Comfort yourself with the thought that all those proverbs like 'A stitch in time' and so on are correct, so that your toil will pay dividends later. The other comfort is that, if you have not toiled, it is not an absolute disaster. For instant satisfaction, cut the hedge.

DECEMBER

Your basic interest in gardening and plants will tell you what to do this month. Your energy and conscience will dictate your achievements. Can we suggest a few ideas for armchair reflection? You may not achieve them all now, but you can next December.

Christmas looms, that most expensive of celebrations, and with forethought and cunning your windowsill, cold frame and garden can save you a fortune. The gift of a carefully chosen plant or its product suggests that you have given the receiver's taste not only a lot of thought, but time as well.

The first task is to divide your friends and relations – everyone to whom you are obliged to give a present – into two broad groups. The 'knows' and the 'don't knows' – that is, the ones that you suspect have more gardening knowledge than you have, and the others. Start with the latter: they are easier.

Subdivide not so much by age and gender as by attitude. Do they love you or regard you as a wimp? There is another subdivision: relations with money on the wimp side should be given special treatment.

'DON'T KNOWS': WIMP DIVISION

Rich Aunties A very small cyclamen, in flower, that you have grown on from a tiny bulb produced by your prize specimen.

Rich Uncles Some sloe berries, picked from a hedge somewhere, preferably soaking in gin.

Others A pot of parsley for the kitchen windowsill. It won't improve your image, but it costs virtually nothing.

'DON'T KNOWS': LOVE DIVISION

Cuttings of shrubs if they have a garden, of geraniums if not. They will feel obliged to keep them alive, and if they grow on and flower well, you will have established a constant reminder of your existence.

'KNOWS'

The good gardeners are much more difficult. The subdivisions of love and wimp will not work. However, cunning will suffice.

Most Difficult Anyone with a prize-winning allotment should be presented with one – only one – of your most presentable parsnips. This shows that you acknowledge their expertise, and indirectly seek their advice.

Indoor Experts For those with a wonderful collection of houseplants, a rooted cutting from your clematis, even if it is only common or garden montana, is just right. This can be grown in a tub if they haven't got a garden. Their pride will ensure its survival, and you may eventually get the satisfaction of seeing it in flower and covering half the house. Do not expect any credit.

Outdoor Experts You might impress with alstroemerias grown from seed. This demonstrates that you have been through all the palaver of putting them in the fridge for a fortnight, etc. etc. Better still, give an unusual houseplant like a silk oak. If your card includes the information that you don't know how tall it will grow, whether it will stand low light levels, or whether or not to pinch out the tip, you will have put your overbearing father- or mother-in-law, uncle, aunt or neighbour on their mettle. As you will have grown half a dozen other specimens yourself, you can experiment, and put the best one on show when the recipient comes to tea.

You will be astonished at how many people will be pleased with your presents. Your nephew with purple hair is quite likely to be secretly delighted with the responsibility of looking after a begonia!

It may also be an idea to spread your largesse beyond Christmas. Take a plant to the party; you only risk the possibility that your hosts neglect it, it dies and they don't invite you again because they cannot put it on show.

JANUARY

VEGETABLE PATCH

Get on with digging, unless the soil is very wet. Dig in as much manure and compost as you can lay your hands on. With heavy soils particularly, frost will break up those weighty clods much more effectively than any mechanical instrument, so finishing digging is *urgent*. Old brassica stumps harbour pests and disease, as do a lot of other decaying bits of rubbish and weeds, so have a good clear up.

Planning the year's crop is more fun than you might think. Draw a plan, and aim to grow what you like best. Runner beans, new potatoes, leeks, calabrese and salad crops head our list; they yield well and save money.

Don't forget next winter: savoy cabbages, swedes, carrots, parsnips, onions should be on the list, but there is little point in buying seeds you have no room to grow.

Having made your selection, buy the seeds, read the instructions on the packet, and sow when it says so.

Bend a leaf over broccoli tops to protect from frost.

If you have not already done so (see 'November'), it is still not too late to upturn a box or bucket over rhubarb to force an early crop. If the plant is getting tired, divide and replant the smaller buds and roots from the outside of the crown in plenty of compost.

With a fork, gently loosen root vegetables that are in the ground before frost gets them in its vice-like grip.

LAWN

Leave the lawn alone: you will be sick of it before midsummer. But if you have nothing better to do, lumps and hollows can be flattened out. Lift the turf in slices at least 2in. (5cm) thick and level off, filling hollows with soil and coarse sand, then replace the turves. Bang them down with the flat of the spade.

FLOWER BEDS & BORDERS

With a gentle boot, firm soil lifted by frost around wallflowers, sweet Williams and any new plantings. This is a job for February and March as well. To protect from frost, mulch (cover with 1 or 2in. (2.5 or 5cm) of compost) paeonies, delphiniums and globe artichokes (a handsome border plant that you can eat!). Tidy up any soggy and diseased-looking leaves, especially round and on roses.

Just as for vegetables, there is some heavy but pleasant armchair planning to be done: what seeds to buy, annual and perennial, and where to grow them.

Again, if the instructions on a seed packet of your choice say sow them, then do it, but if you cannot provide ideal conditions, don't worry. Most plants are good at catching up when sown late in good conditions; the real folly is sowing too early.

Clear up weeds – they harbour pests – and dig where the annual flowers will go. As everywhere else, the more muck or compost you get into the soil, the better its structure will be, and the better the plants you'll grow.

HOUSEPLANTS, WINDOW BOXES, TUBS & TROUGHS

Continue to watch the watering. Most houseplants need very little water, and hardly any feeding in winter. *Do not* leave plants on the windowsill behind the curtains at night.

If you have troughs and tubs planted with alpines, make sure that the surface grit is tucked in under the leaves to help drainage. If the containers hold spring bulbs or shrubs – or both – mulch with compost or peat.

FRUIT TREES & BUSHES

The professionals spray with tar oil now, but remember that this kills *all* bugs, the good and the bad. If there were a lot of pests about last year, best to do it, but *on a still day*.

Prune for shape and to let light in to all parts. Remember that this encourages spring growth, so you can be brutal with young trees. Cut back to just above a bud.

It is still a good time to buy and plant. Remember that bare-rooted trees are cheaper than those grown in containers. Buy them from the garden centre when the soil is not too wet, nor frosty, and get them in immediately.

WINDOWSILL, COLD FRAME & GREENHOUSE

The hesitant gardener starts growing seeds in the airing cupboard, then rears them on the windowsill. With a little success he, or more often she, gets enthusiastic and finds that there are not enough windowsills. A cold frame comes next, easy and cheap to make,

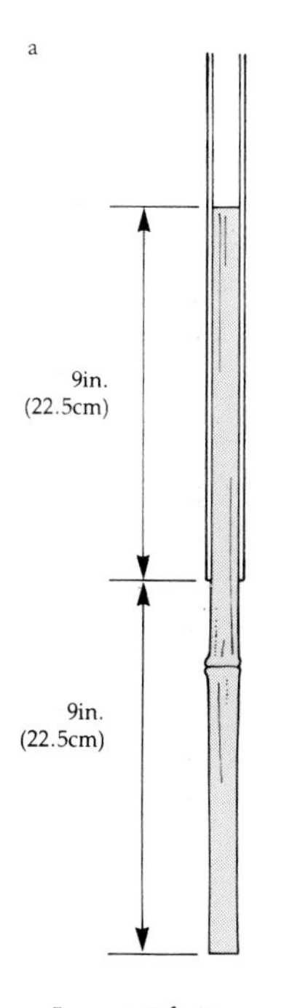

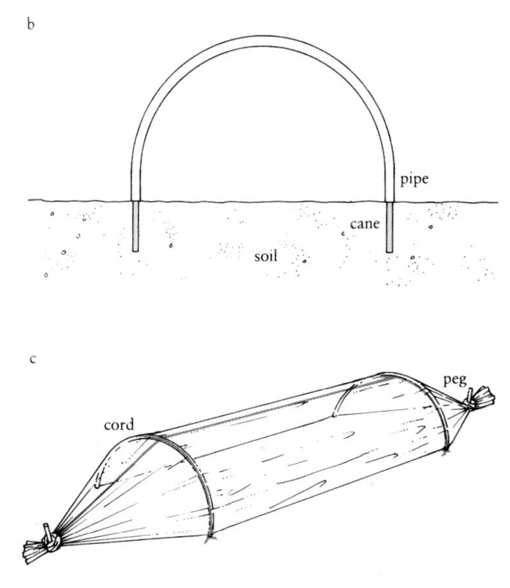

a *Insert 1ft 6in. (45cm) cane 9in. (22.5cm) into water pipe*

b *Bend water pipe to make hoop*

c *Cover with polythene, securing with pegs and cord*

using garden cane, ¾in. (2cm) water pipe (*not* garden hose), cord and polythene. That helps for a while. Then there is nothing for it but to give up smoking to buy a greenhouse. Growing plants is easy, and very satisfying, as long as it is regarded as the art of the possible. Seedlings must have plenty of light, and be protected from frost. So if you have only the windowsill, choose your January sowings to fill the space available and give up smoking at once.

Leeks, onions, cabbages and cauliflowers

can be sown in pots and trays, as can begonias, geraniums and gloxinias if you want some good houseplants. (You don't need many plants, and seed is expensive, so share with a friend. Competing to see who grows the best plants adds a bit of spice to the business.)

Sweet pea buffs sow seeds in October, but now is the time for ordinary mortals. Sow in the top ½in. (1cm) of a toilet roll, for they grow long roots. It's not worth trying them, however, if you do not have a sunny spot outside to grow the adult plants in.

Alpine seeds and those of many trees and shrubs can be sown now, but they don't need to crowd the windowsill: they go outside in the frost to break their dormancy.

If you have an unheated greenhouse, buy a cheap propagator (about £6). It will pay for itself over and over again in the first year. As the seeds germinate, the pots or trays can be moved to make way for the next lot. To keep the frost off, make a low polythene frame as cheaply as possible from wire and bits of wood, and put the propagator inside. The heat that leaks out of it will keep the temperature above zero. It will not provide a perfect climate for the seedlings, but they will survive. Lift the frame off by day unless it is very cold.

TREES, SHRUBS & CLIMBERS

As with fruit, it is still a good time to put in new ornamental trees and shrubs, so long as the ground is unfrozen and not wet and sticky.

New trees and young trees need staking well (see page 18). Check the ties on all of them: they should be firm enough to avoid rubbing when the wind blows, but not so tight that they cut into the bark. As the tree grows, the stake and tie need to be watched carefully. Except for large specimens, a low stake is ideal. It is not at all unsightly, and the trunk gains strength from bending in the wind.

Do not be in a hurry to remove supports,

WHAT ARE ROOTSTOCKS?

All top fruit is grafted on to a particular rootstock which affects the ultimate size and vigour of the tree. Rootstocks you are likely to encounter are:

M27 for trees under 6ft (1.8m) high, fruiting in two or three years. Needs good soil and careful treatment.

M9 for trees of about 6–8ft (1.8–2.4m) which fruit in about three years. Again needs good soil and careful treatment.

M26 produces a still larger tree which fruits in about four years but requires staking for at least five years.

MM106 Many consider this to be the best rootstock for the average garden. It produces a larger tree than M26, cropping in about five years.

MM111 Very vigorous but takes about eight years to fruit. Good for a poor soil.

even if you don't like the look of them. Wait three or four years at least.

Cut off damaged and diseased branches, and make a tidy, clean job of it, flush to the trunk or close to a healthy bud. Knock the snow off evergreens, then go back to that armchair, get out the catalogues and think about winter colour. You might decide to replace that boring misshapen thing that you inherited with a real specimen.

If you have a choice shrub that is a bit tender, try to protect it from cold winds and frost. Straw, bracken and hessian screens all work: you will have to use ingenuity.

GENERAL

If you have done the digging, and sown all the seeds you can accommodate, just concentrate on planning.

If you did not do it back in November, cutting the hedge brings a glow to the cheeks on a frosty day; and the goldfish will be grateful if you melt the ice on the pond – not by bashing it, but by placing a pan full of hot water on top, and melting a few holes gently.

Clean everything. Dirty pots and seed trays can carry over disease; weeds and detritus sustain pests as well. Spray the cloches, cold frame and greenhouse with Jeyes' fluid.

STORING VEGETABLES AND FRUIT

BY CLAY JONES

At some time or other most gardeners find themselves with a surplus of garden produce, despite careful pre-planning. Fruit trees, for instance, have lean years and fat years depending on factors such as weather conditions at flowering time, and whether the trees are biennial bearers. So, for one reason or another, we reach the end of the season with an embarrassment of riches and a desire to preserve the surplus rather than let it go to waste. The advent of deep freezers has eased the storage problem, but even they have a limited capacity and, in any case, there are many vegetables and fruits that are either unsuitable for freezing or are better stored under natural conditions.

As in gardening generally, there are few hard and fast rules, but there are a few helpful guidelines. I have always recognised that the easiest things to store are those that nature intended to be stored. Take carrots, for instance: they and many other root crops are biennial. In other words, they have every intention of completing a two-year life cycle. In the first year after sowing they concentrate on growth and the food produced in the leaves is fed back down to the roots, which become food-storage organs rather than merely anchors and liquid absorbers. If these roots are left in the ground over winter, they will initiate new growth in the spring for the express purpose of producing flowers and eventually seeds, thus ensuring the continued existence of the species. Therefore, overwinter storage is their way of life and all they need from us to remain pure and palatable is a little help.

The fruits and vegetables that require the greatest care and ingenuity in store are those with an annual rather than a biennial life pattern. As far as they are concerned, they are fully prepared to die at the end of the growing season, leaving their seeds behind to perpetuate their kind by germinating in the spring of the following year. Their storage life is limited and storage can only be attained, within limits, by providing ideal keeping conditions.

These conditions apply not only to the annuals but also to the biennials and are all based on the principle of deep dormancy. The trick is to keep the fruits and vegetables in such a comatose condition that they have no desire to grow, yet neither are they inclined to rot and perish. The first essential is to keep them cool at a temperature that is low enough to inhibit growth, but not so low that their tissues will suffer permanent damage. So they need a cold shed, garage or cellar that is frost-proof and in which the temperature is fairly uniform and does not rise dramatically on sunny winter days. Second, they need surrounding air that is neither too dry nor too damp. In a dry atmosphere fruits and vegetables lose moisture rapidly, their tissues contract or, as the saying goes, they 'go sleepy'; whereas when the surrounding air is overdamp, the produce is wide open to all kinds of fungus diseases that induce rotting. Third and finally, the best storage conditions are those that also exclude light. So there it is: keep your autumn harvest cool, moist and in darkness and you will enjoy the fresh flavour of home-grown produce right through the winter months.

The afore-mentioned storage conditions apply to all fruits and vegetables, but there are, as always, different ways and means of achieving the ideal. Very often gardeners have found, by trial and error, that certain kinds of crops respond better to certain methods of storage than others. I can only explain more fully by dealing with each fruit and vegetable individually or in groups within their respective families.

ROOT CROPS

Included in the root-crop class are carrots, beetroot, parsnips, swedes, turnips and potatoes, although the latter are actually swollen stems rather than distended roots. For the sake of convenience I group them all together.

Potato storage was once laborious; now it isn't. In days of old, maincrop potatoes were lifted and stored in 'clamps'. An area of ground was covered with straw, a layer of potatoes was placed on it, these were strawed over, followed by another layer of potatoes and so on until a sizeable mound was achieved. As building progressed, the sides of the mound were encased in a thickness of soil, and when it reached its peak it was top-sealed with more soil. Nowadays few of us grow enough potatoes to warrant 'clamping' and, in any event, there is a much easier way.

On a dry day when the haulms (green tops) of the potatoes have died completely, lift the tubers and leave them on the soil surface for two or three hours to dry. When they are dry, rub off most of the soil and put the tubers into brown paper or hessian sacks and tie the tops. You can get the sacks second-hand for nothing, if you are on good terms with your greengrocer. I stress that the sacks must be either hessian or brown paper and not plastic: in plastic bags the potatoes sweat and rot, and in clear plastic they will assimilate light, turn green and become not only unpalatable but also poisonous.

It is also worth noting that not all maincrop potato varieties reach cropping maturity at the same time. Golden Wonder, for example, retains its green haulms quite a bit longer than King Edward and usually it is not ready for 'the lift' until the third or fourth week of October.

Carrots lose moisture more rapidly than potatoes and tend to shrivel if stored in sacks, but there are several ways of keeping them in prime condition until the following April. One way is to leave them in the ground until October, then lift them, clean off excess soil (but don't wash them), remove the leaves just above the crown and store them in boxes or buckets as follows. Place a layer of slightly moist sand or peat in the bottom, put a top-to-tail layer of carrots on top and follow on with alternate layers of sand or peat and carrots. However, for the past

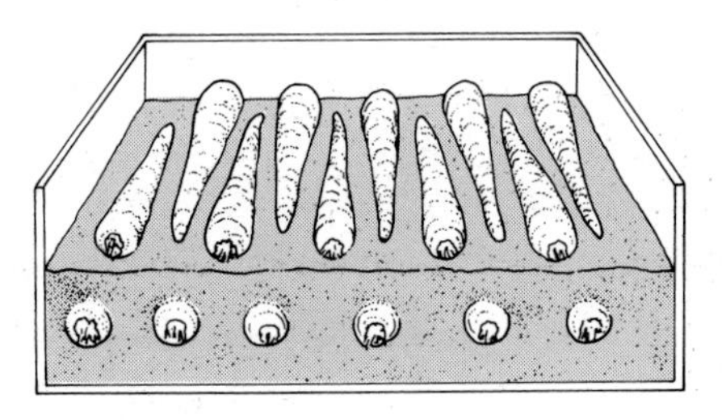

Storing carrots

few years I haven't bothered to lift my carrots – I've left them in the ground, scattered a few slug pellets along the rows and covered them with cloches. They have survived some low temperatures and have remained in harvest-fresh condition until they began sprouting leaves in late March. I'm not sure whether this *in situ* storage would work as well on a heavy clay soil that tends to get waterlogged, but it's worth trying.

Beetroot are less hardy than carrots and need undercover storage. Fork the roots up before the first hard frosts, screw the leaves off at the crown, hand clean them and store them in layers of sand or peat.

Swedes and turnips are hard-centred, thick-skinned and, like potatoes, they store well in paper sacks. Parsnips are the easiest of all. They are as tough as TV cameramen and are undaunted by winter's worst; in fact, the more they are frosted, the sweeter they are! So leave them in the ground.

All members of the onion family are good storers. One way or another, I can keep onions, shallots and garlic in prime condition almost until the new season's crop is ready for harvest.

Garlic is the first to mature. Here in the south the leaves brown off some time in July and this means that the bulbs are ready for lifting. Put a fork or a trowel under them, ease them out of the ground and rub off as much soil as you can. Leave the tops on and put the bulbs somewhere warm and dry to finish ripening, preferably in the sun. Never leave them out in rain as it gets under the outer parchment-thin layer of skin and rot may set in. When you are satisfied that they are fully dry, tie the old stems together in bundles and hang them somewhere cool and dry.

Shallots come next, indicating their readiness for lifting by their withered leaves. Fork them out and leave the bulbs in their clumps, either on dry soil or on the path for a few days to harden their skins. Then prise the individual bulbs apart, spread them on sheets of newspaper on a sunny windowsill and leave them until their outer skins are hard and dry. Any bits of loose skin should be rubbed off. Some gardeners advocate leaving the shallot bulbs out in the open on a wire-netting frame, but in our uncertain summers I prefer to take them indoors after the initial weather exposure. If you intend to use them fairly quickly for pickles, the bulbs can take a few showers of rain with no noticeable effect. If they are required for long keeping, however, you will find that the rain has softened their skins and worked its way between the layers and they tend to go mouldy in store.

And so to onions. With so much care and devotion lavished on growing these beautiful, delicious bulbs, it is vital that they be harvested correctly. Somewhere about the middle to the end of August some of the leaves will begin to flop over, and at this stage some books tell you to nip down the rows bending all the leaves down to the ground. In my experience all this achieves is tidy-looking rows. Bending upstanding leaves bruises them at the neck, and in a wet summer the damaged area is an open invitation to neck rot fungus that will develop later in store.

The best course is to wait until some leaves begin to look limp and then to put a fork under each onion and lever it up gently, until you can feel some of the roots snapping. Halt, don't lift them any further! With the broken roots still in the soil, the leaves will gradually keel over and it is then, and only then, that the leaves can be turned inwards, alternating the turning from right to left in adjacent rows. Now leave well alone for two weeks and then lift the bulbs and lay them on their sides with their bottoms facing south into the sun. As you lift, clean off the

HOW MUCH LAND DO I OWN?

1 acre/4,840 square yards (0.4 hectare) or about the size of a small football pitch.

½acre/2,420 square yards (0.2 hectare).

1/10 acre/484 square yards (0.04 hectare), about the size of the penalty area.

soil and gently remove any loose outer skin. The drying and ripening process is vital and the bulbs should not be exposed to rain for any length of time.

Keen onion addicts go to the trouble of constructing 2ft (60cm) tall, rectangular, wooden frames topped with 1in. (2.5cm) mesh wire netting. They drop the leaves down through the wire, leaving the bulbs high and dry with their bottoms facing skywards. I just take them into the greenhouse and leave them on the staging with their 'tails' hanging down over the edge.

Onions may be stored in several ways. They may be strung in 'ropes',

Storing onions by tying them on to a rope

or they may be contained in old nylon stockings or polythene netting. I do neither, as in both methods the bulbs are in very close contact, and should one be diseased, it passes its sickness on to its neighbours. I achieve a high storage success rate by simply cutting off the withered leaves just above the shoulder of the bulbs and storing them, bottom up, in single layers in shallow boxes or trays, which are then kept in a cold but frost-proof attic. The onions keep in tip-top condition until early May.

Cabbages do not store well and as there are winter-maturing varieties, it is hardly worth trying. However, the variety Winter White can be stored and used as a reserve, should the outdoor ones be lost. Seed is sown in June and the plants are lifted with their roots intact in October. Their loose outer leaves are stripped off and the heads are hung in a cold but frost-free shed or garage. I have found that I can also store autumn cauliflowers for a few weeks by this method.

Tomatoes too have a limited storage life. Ripe ones will hardly keep at all, although their edible life can be extended by several days by keeping them in the bottom box compartment of the refrigerator – not the freezer. End-of-season green tomatoes are another matter. Some I make into lip-smacking green tomato chutney; with the others I cut off the whole trusses and hang them from wires strung across the cold attic. When we need a few, I take a truss into the warmth of the kitchen and in a week or two they ripen nicely. By this method we enjoy our home-grown tomatoes right up to December.

Marrows will keep for months if they are cut in September and stored somewhere reasonably dry, cold and protected from frost.

Many herbs will overwinter successfully in the open, but if in doubt a few sprigs may be cut in June and then hung in bunches to dry in a cool airy place.

In the old cottages it was a familiar sight to see numerous brown paper bags hanging from the beams along with sides of salted pork. They contained a variety of dried herbs, protecting them from dust, and these were used as the need arose. Nowadays fresh herbs can be finely minced and then frozen in ice cubes and stored in the freezer.

Finally, a few lines on fruit. Soft fruit does not store, although currants, gooseberries and raspberries freeze very well, and of the stone fruits only apples and pears are suitable for long storage.

In the 'big houses' of old there were custom-made storage rooms for apples and pears which were dark, cool and frost-proof and where the air was not too dry. Modern gardens do not yield enough fruit to warrant such extravagance, but there is an easy way of emulating the necessary storage conditions.

Obtain a supply of clear polythene bags, each big enough to hold about 7lb (3kg) of fruit. Fill each one, tie the necks tightly, puncture the sides with five or six holes of pencil thickness and, ideally, hang them somewhere like a cold attic or shed, where frost won't damage them. Remember, though, that they must be late-maturing varieties that are suitable for storing. In general, apples and pears that ripen in August, September and October should be eaten either 'off the tree' or within a very short time of picking.

I have left two important maxims to the very end. First store only undamaged, disease-free produce. Second, examine the stored produce regularly and throw out anything that is not still fit.

WHAT IS A SPIT?

The depth of a spade blade.

HOW MUCH GRAVEL FOR A PATH?

Gravel is usually sold by the cubic yard, so at a rate of 2 to 3in. of gravel, 1 cubic yard of gravel will cover between 12 and 18 square yards.

PAVING AND WALLS

BY GEOFF HAMILTON

Laying paving and building walls is called 'hard landscaping' because of the nature of the materials. But the adjective could also apply to the work itself, for no one could deny that it's not a job for the faint-hearted. Hard work it certainly is, so all the more reason for getting it right first time.

This really is the one area in the building of a new garden where it's folly to take short cuts. If you do, you'll find that your patio is swimming in water or that it sinks unevenly, creating dangerous 'trips'. Even worse, you could end up with the sitting-room wallpaper peeling off damp walls. However, if you take your time and do it right, you'll thoroughly enjoy it and you'll save yourself a small fortune.

PAVING

For modern houses as well as old, there's no doubt that rectangular paving is much the best material to use for your patio or path.

There is a very wide range to choose from these days, from the rather 'municipal-looking' grey square slab to reconstituted stone paving of all shapes, sizes and finishes. There will certainly be a finish to suit your house. Crazy paving is cheap but pretty nasty in the garden of a modern house; in my view, it should only be used in a real country cottage garden.

It's quite likely that you'll want to lay the paving in a 'random' pattern, using several sizes of slabs to create a more informal effect. If you do, ordering the paving can be tricky. Either work out a pattern before you order or, if you prefer a really random effect worked out as you go along, make sure that you order equal areas of the different sizes. If you ask for equal numbers, you'll finish up with far too many large ones. Even then, be prepared to go back to the supplier when you near the end, to change the odd couple of slabs which you can't fit in.

Marking Out

Check the sizes of the materials available even before you start to design the patio. It will save a lot of arduous cutting if you make the size and shape of the paved area to fit the size of the paving. Remember that most slabs are now in metric sizes which, if you're laying several, will make a difference of a few inches if you've worked out the design in imperial measurements.

Bang in the first peg near the wall

The second row of pegs should be slightly lower than the first

In the garden, start by marking out the shape of the paved area with pegs.

If the patio is to be adjacent to the house, as most are, it will need to finish at least two courses of bricks below the damp-proof course (DPC). This ensures that water does not splash up above it and start to creep in and up the wall. You can recognise the DPC easily on modern houses because the mortar between the bricks is much thicker there. On older houses it may be a course of dark blue engineering bricks or there may not, of course, be a DPC at all.

Having located the correct level, roughly dig out the soil until it's about three courses of bricks below the DPC. Then put in pegs to make absolutely sure you've got it right. The top of the pegs should finish at the finish level of the paving, but before banging them in, mark a line 3in. (7.5cm) from the top if you are using 2in. (5cm) thick slabs and 2½in. (6.3cm) if they are 1½in. (3.8cm) thick. This line will show you where to bring the concrete base. It allows for the thickness of the slab plus 1in. (2.5cm) of mortar for setting it.

Bang in the first peg near the wall and, using a spirit-level, make sure the top comes level with the top of the course of bricks two below the DPC. Then, using this peg as a guide, put in a row along the wall.

Obviously, the patio must slope very slightly away from the house to ensure that rain water runs off, so the next row of pegs slightly further from the wall must be a bit lower than the first row. Do this by placing a ½in. (1cm) block of wood on top of the peg when levelling from the pegs in the first row. Remove the block and the pegs will all be ½in. (1cm) lower. If you need a third row, the same principle applies.

Now ensure that you have dug out enough soil to allow a bed of concrete at least 3in. (7.5cm) deep. High patches can be scraped out a little, but avoid re-filling low spots with soil. It's better to do this with either broken bricks or rubble, or with concrete.

The Base

This is where many folk skimp a bit and, believe me, it really is a false economy, especially if the house is newly built. In that case, the footings will have been dug out with an oversized mechanical shovel. The concrete is put in, the walls are built and then the trench is re-filled.

It always takes a considerable time for that soil to sink. And when it does, your newly laid paving will sink with it. Only if the soil has been consolidated over several years is it safe to reduce the amount of concrete used for the base. But you can still make it easy on yourself.

Mix up 6 parts of ¾in. (2cm) 'all-in' ballast (that's a mixture of sharp sand and gravel) with 1 part of cement, but mix it dry. Spread it out over the site and level it so that the top of the concrete comes level with the mark on the pegs you made previously. Then tread it down hard with your heels and level again. It doesn't matter too much if you're a little bit low, because you can make that up with mortar later, but if you're too high, you could be in trouble when it comes to levelling the slabs. There's no need to wet the concrete at all. Moisture seeping up from below and rain from above will soon harden it off.

Laying the Slabs

The slabs are laid on a bed of mortar made with builder's sand and cement. Mix it up at 3 parts of sand to 1 part of cement and make sure that it's not too sloppy. You need very little water, in fact, because there will be a tendency for the mortar to slump if it's too wet.

Rest the first slab on the mortar, then tap to make level with peg

Start with the first slab about 1in. (2.5cm) away from the wall. Lay out five small piles of mortar about 3in. (7.5cm) or so high, so that there will be one at each corner of the slab and one in the middle. Now rest the slab on top and make sure it's straight with the house wall. You can do this with a bricklayer's line running from the inside edge of the slab to the end of the wall and again about 1in. (2.5cm) away from it. The slab should line up with the bricklayer's line.

Now, to make sure it's level, put the spirit-level from the slab to the top of the nearest peg. Tap down the slab with the handle (never the head) of a club-hammer until it lies level with the top of the peg. Then check the levels from the other pegs just to make quite sure. It's well

With the first slab in place, the remaining slabs can now be laid

worthwhile checking very regularly to ensure that the slabs are running level.

Then lay out another five piles of mortar as before, right next to the first slab, and repeat the process. The second slab should be butted right up against the first to avoid pointing in between. The only exception to this rule is where you wish to brush soil between the slabs to accommodate alpine plants.

The remainder of the slabs are then laid in exactly the same way. If you're working out a random style as you go along, you'll have to think a couple of slabs ahead. The idea is to avoid long 'tramlines', so if a line looks as though it's getting too long, break it by putting a slab across it.

When you've finished laying all the slabs, all you need do is to point in between the first row of slabs and the house wall.

Cutting Paving

If you're blessed with an inspection cover in the middle of your new patio, as most of us are (I once laid one in where there were five!), you'll almost certainly have to cut some slabs to fit.

Though this can be done with a little trial and error using a brick or a stone bolster and a hammer, there's no doubt that the easiest way is with a saw. You can hire an angle-grinder from the small-tool hire shop. Ask for a stone-cutting disc or – if you have more than a couple of dozen slabs to cut – two, because they wear out pretty fast.

WALLING

It's generally possible to buy artificial stone walling to match the paving, and naturally they look good together. But building with stone, either natural or artificial, differs a little from bricklaying. The reason is that the face of stone walling is not smooth like that of brick, so wet mortar will stick to it, leaving ugly marks. It's therefore essential to mix the mortar much drier than the sloppy mix you'll see brickies using.

Use a 3 to 1 mix of builder's sand and masonry cement, and mix it dry enough not to stick to the stones.

The other problem with an uneven face is that you can't put a spirit-level vertically on the face of the wall to check that it's not leaning. You must, therefore, rely on a straight bricklayer's line and a good eye.

The Footings

The footings should always be at least twice the width of the intended wall and 4in. (10cm) deep for a wall three courses high. Higher walls will need thicker footings.

Start by digging out a trench along the line of the wall and then bang in some level pegs. Using the spirit-level, set them so that they come just

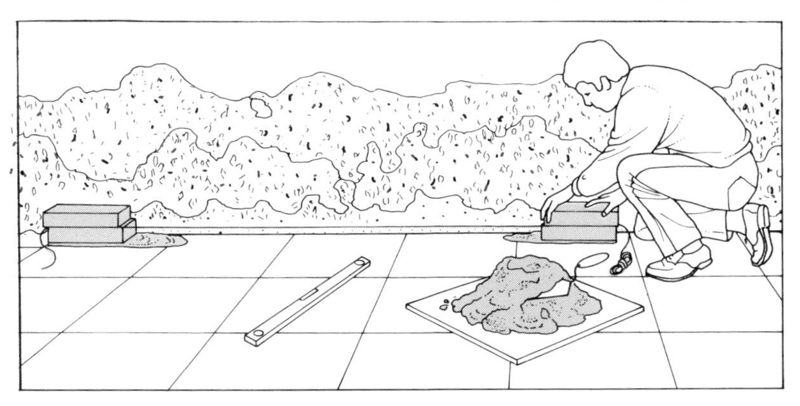

Hold the bricklayer's line in place with loose stones

below soil level or, if the wall is adjacent to paving, about ½in. (1cm) below that. Fill in with wet concrete made using a 6:1 mix of ballast and cement.

Laying the Stones

Start by setting a stone at each end of the run of walling. Lay it on about ½in. (1cm) of mortar and tap it down level with the handle of a club-hammer. Then run a bricklayer's line from stone to stone, setting it so that it runs along the top front edge of the stones. Hold it in place by anchoring the ends round a spare stone and position it on the top of the laid stones by resting another stone on top of it. This will then give you both the line and the level of the other stones in that course. When you lay these, leave a gap of about ½in. (1cm) between each stone and point them in with mortar when the whole course is finished.

The second and subsequent courses are laid in exactly the same way, except that the stones will need to be 'bonded'. That means that you start each alternate course with half a stone so that each joint is overlapped by a stone above it, just like a brick wall.

At the end of each day, when the mortar has set but not hardened completely, rake out the joints by scraping any excess mortar back with a piece of wood. Then brush the face of the wall clean to remove any mortar that may be lodged on it.

Copings

Bear in mind that a coping is necessary on top of the wall, in order to shed water. Otherwise it may get into the joints and the stone during the winter when frost action may cause cracking. Most suppliers will be able to sell you a matching coping, which is simply set on top of the stones so that it overlaps the face of the wall by about 1in. (2.5cm).

GARDEN VISITING

BY ASHLEY STEPHENSON

We are a race of gardeners and as such, no matter the size of our plot, we are always striving for perfection. This I consider is the main reason why we visit gardens. For the many visitors who have no gardens at all there is still a desire to see colour and form in a setting which enhances its surroundings. There are few people who are left unmoved when encountering a display of riotous colour which has been set into the frame of the surrounding landscape.

Design is the first element which hits the senses: no matter how well planted a garden may be, if this is not a part of the construction much is lost. Throughout the country there are thousands of gardens to visit, some many acres in extent, others quite small and much nearer the size of the normal detached house garden. Each has much to offer; it is only by visiting that we are able to obtain ideas, which can then be transported to our own gardens.

Garden visiting is a fairly recent phenomenon. It was not until the motor car became an every-day means of travel that large numbers of the public started visiting. Parks and municipal open spaces had always been used by the 'locals' but, apart from some of the better-known London parks, there was no real migration to them by the tourists. Large estates were the breeding grounds of today's gardeners, and it was there that the experience and knowledge of the legendary head gardeners were transferred to the young journeymen just starting on their careers. Many of these large estates employed dozens of gardeners and it was not difficult for a man to build up a wealth of knowledge by moving from garden to garden.

There are few gardens now where the number of staff exceeds double figures, except where the garden has been taken over by an organisation such as the National Trust or by a multi-national company. Training is more difficult, but as the estates slowly diminished in number and size, parks departments have increased their potential for introducing skilled labour into horticulture. Many impressive gardens come under the control of the local authority or of central government.

Our gardening heritage has built up since the earliest of our present-day large gardens were laid down in the seventeenth century and onwards. The gardens of Hampton Court, for instance, have remained almost intact, from a design point of view, since they were first established all those years ago. Many other gardens, although not dating as far back as that of Hampton Court, can show their origins in our history, and it is this factor which makes the pastime of garden visiting so fascinating. However, modern gardens also have much to commend them and they should not be discounted because they are young. In many cases they are, of course, more relevant to the private house dweller than the grounds of Blenheim Palace.

Plant hunting has been going on for some centuries but it was not until the eighteenth and nineteenth centuries that the wealth of plant material which we know so well was introduced. Garden design changed somewhat to accommodate the new plants which were all the rage. Victorian bedding schemes were massive and very ornate, and it was about this time that the heated greenhouse came into use for plants other than vines and peaches. Collections of plants can be found in gardens all over the country and it is from mature specimens that the true worth of a plant is recognised.

The more we visit, the more apparent it becomes that there has to be a structure on which a garden is designed. It is this structure planting which enables the garden to be laid out to suit one's own needs. Smaller plots usually require the structure planting to be placed round the perimeter of the garden; larger plots, of necessity, have to have the body of the garden built up of mature plants to provide that sense of maturity which is the background to all else we do.

On visiting a new garden for the first time, there should be a feeling of anticipation, and the first thing to strike should be the design. Does it feel as though the garden has been stuck on to the house? The initial impression is the one to trust, particularly if you are looking for inspiration for your own garden.

I am a plantsman and the overriding reason why I visit gardens is to look at plants. I want to see what my fellows have decided is the best plant to fit a variety of situations. There are always parts of one's own garden which can be a problem, and so often someone else has already solved it.

The siting of trees or other plants which act as an exclamation mark in the garden is most difficult to achieve. They have to stand out from their surroundings, yet at the same time be part of them. The type, size and formation of such specimens must be carefully selected, and seeing them in their natural habitat gives the broadest hint yet as to how they can best be fitted into a garden scheme. Any specimen planting, however, needs some experience in siting; it is only by knowing the plants concerned that this can be done successfully from the beginning. Britain has a very wide range of trees which are suitable for most types of garden with sufficient space and so long as you take into account the soil conditions and the trees' hardiness. Gardens open to the public are the best sources of information available on this subject. From your own observations it is easy to tell if you can adapt your selections to fit the individual conditions of your own plot.

Soil conditions I would bracket with plant hardiness when you are looking for ideas. No matter what part of the country your garden is in, there will be gardens which have the same conditions as yours and from which you can gain ideas. Assess plant hardiness by observing what is growing in these gardens and try to relate it to the positions you wish to plant. Plants such as *Acacia dealbata* will be difficult to establish in Yorkshire or Northumberland, for example, but grow perfectly well on the south coast and Isle of Wight. Remember the positions in which you observed tender and half-hardy trees planted, as very often it is not the cold which kills but a cold drying wind on a plant set in wet poorly drained land.

'Soil pH' indicates acidity or alkalinity. If gardening on chalk, do not attempt to grow plants which will not tolerate this. Acid soils are ideal for some plants, but remember that the most successful gardens are those which cater for the conditions on site, and that within the thousands of gardens open to visitors there are a great many specialist gardens. It is relatively simple to select from the lists available (see page 146) which ones would be most beneficial for you to visit – which would help you most with your own particular problems.

The garden-visiting public is aware of the need to visit gardens over a period, as different gardens look their best at different times of the year and one single garden may have several 'peaks'. Gardeners like something of interest in the garden over as long a period as possible. The best way to see plants grown in association with others and to consider their interest is to see how they have been planted in the well-known and well-maintained gardens. Soil conditions in the garden change as the seasons change and it is important only to plant in wet or moist situations plants which will accept these conditions. Shade is another factor to be taken into account, and it is vital to know that there are a number of solutions to the problem this poses, all of which can be found when visiting other gardens.

Bedding out is probably more popular now than it has ever been, even more than during the last century when it was beloved by the Victorians. The famous gardens of today still practise bedding out on a large scale, and it is in these that you will see the mixing and blending of colour, how to use edging as well as dot plants, and how to fit in specimens. You will also see the new varieties, which are usually grown commercially before they appear on the general market. New colours or combinations of colour are always worth spending time over.

Garden visiting will therefore provide you with a reservoir of ideas on how to prepare and/or develop sections of your own garden. You will discover where to see trees and shrubs which take some time to become typical, and learn to assess how they will fit into your own plot; you will get to know the idiosyncrasies of individual plants so that their situation in your garden can be selected to take account of soil as well as temperature; you will have at your recall a list of names and aspects so you will be able to plant the best when the need arises.

Below I describe my ten favourite gardens in Britain – a difficult choice. They are nationally based and not confined to the warmer climes of the south and south-east.

BETH CHATTO GARDENS

Elmstead Market, Colchester, Essex

Beth Chatto Gardens are between 3 and 4 acres (1.2 and 1.6 hectares) in area. They lie in a hollow and contain some fine oaks which act as cover and shade to the plants beneath. The design of the garden is such that it appears a great deal bigger than its true size, open areas of lawn setting off the beautifully planted borders. There are no straight lines, only soft flowing curves which are not only pleasing to the eye, but also assist greatly with maintenance.

This is a plantsman's garden, full of unusual and interesting plants looking their best in sites in which they would grow naturally. There are plants for hot dry places as well as plants for cool wet positions, with almost all the intermediate stages. *Cytisus battandieri* is but one of the different shrubby plants which act as a background to the perennials for which this garden is famous. *Verbascum olympicum*, at 10ft (3m) tall, makes a bold shape, but then all planting is bold. Hemerocallis, astilbe, achillea, calamintha, iris, crocosmia, heuchera, geranium, euphorbia and phlox are about in abundance, as are primulas by the score, bergenias, hostas and chrysanthemums. It is a garden to be viewed at almost any time of the year.

BODNANT GARDENS

Talycafn, Colwyn Bay, Gwynedd, Wales

A large garden of about 80 acres (32.3 hectares), Bodnant is set into the North Wales landscape where by virtue of its position it is able to provide a setting for many plants which would normally not be suitable for this area of Britain. The soil is basically lime-free, which gives it the opportunity of growing exceptionally well that magnificent genus, *Rhododendron*.

The garden is terraced and, as in all good gardens, there is water. This is used to great advantage, allowing the structure planting to be full and exciting. Cedars provide a maturity to the site which belies their age, and there are many other varieties of trees including *Arbutus andrachnoides*, *Magnolia campbellii* and birches which add the attraction of their white bark (*Betula ermanii* stands out in this company). Beeches supply beautiful autumn colours as well as providing that shimmering look which gives much to the garden.

Rhododendrons can be seen in all their glory. The range of species is enormous and spring into early summer is a time of wonder and delight. Look for *Rhododendron falconeri* and *Rhododendron calophytum* of the big leaves, as well as the azalea types, such as *kaempferi* and *schlippenbachii*. Hardy hybrids are well represented, reaching 8ft (2.4m) and above in height.

CRAGSIDE HOUSE
Rothbury, Northumberland

Northumberland enjoys the scenic beauty of both heathland and low hills. Cragside is situated on the side of a hill on the outskirts of Rothbury. This is not a garden in the same sense as Bodnant, but it has a peace and tranquillity missing in so many of our gardens. In excess of 900 acres (364 hectares), it boasts few large deciduous trees, but has ample space and water to provide an area of beauty.

The area is ideal for coniferous trees and on the lower parts of the estate in particular are a number of fine specimens. They must all be hardy forms for they flourish on the exposed site. Firs abound, some of them in excess of 100ft (30m) high: Douglas, noble and giant fir, as well as the western hemlock and *Tsuga heterophylla*, look vigorous and well.

Woods and moorland make for exciting walking, although you must be well shod. The gardens are ablaze with *Rhododendron ponticum* and *Rhododendron luteum* in the early summer, together with *Gaultheria shallon*, *Pernettya mucronata*, a number of barberries (in particular *Berberis × stenophylla*), and the tall white-plumed *Holodiscus discolor*. Hardy ferns growing in crevices complete a lovely picture.

EAST LAMBROOK MANOR
South Petherton, Somerset

A relatively small garden, East Lambrook nonetheless has had a lasting influence on the gardeners of today as it was here, under the guidance of the late Margery Fish, that ground-cover plants first came into their own. This is not a 'pretty pretty' garden, but the plantsman can still spend many hours browsing here.

Gardening is not necessarily all to do with flower colour, and in a plot where it is difficult to grow plants which demand good light, foliage and form come into their own. At Lambrook Manor a number of plants which are now well-known and highly regarded were seen for the first time. *Artemesia* 'Lambrook Silver', *Euphorbia* 'Lambrook Gold', *Hebe* 'Margery Fish' and *Penstemon* 'Margery Fish' are but a few of these.

This is a garden to visit if you are interested in low-maintenance gardening. Here you can see how each of the plants is reacting to the position in which it is planted. Hellebores are popular plants today but they were first used for underplanting on a large scale by Margery Fish, and Lambrook Manor has one of the biggest collections in the country. Lamiums, ivies in all shapes and sizes, bergenias, hostas and some saxifragas are happy beneath clematis and honeysuckle in this quiet garden.

GREAT DIXTER
Northiam, Sussex

The garden at Great Dixter, formed round a Lutyens designed house set in the countryside some miles from the sea in Sussex, has a different ambience again. It is compiled of small sections which, although each a part of the whole, all have a different feel to them as you meander through. I particularly like the long border, which has become well known for its exciting plant combinations. It is here you can see *Allium neapolitanum*, *Fillipendula ulmaria* 'Aurea', which should not be allowed to flower, *Euphorbia polychroma* and *Euphorbia wulfenii*. Galega makes a large plant and covers a lot of space, and its wisteria-like flowers are a joy. *Sedum* 'Ruby Glow' and *Rudbeckia* 'Goldsturm' are boldly planted, and as the summer progresses there are large colonies of *Anemone japonica*, both white- and pink-flowered.

Roses abound and in the Rose Garden, despite the Sussex propensity to black spot, they flourish. Not many of them are the modern hybrids; they are in the main species roses.

Topiary is almost a forgotten art but there are one or two fine examples here for all to see and to attempt to copy.

HIDCOTE MANOR GARDENS
Chipping Campden, Gloucestershire

Most of the gardens I have described so far have been on acidic or nearly neutral soils; Hidcote, on the other hand, is a garden which is basically alkaline. To those of you who garden on chalk this is a good garden to visit as it is one of the real jewels among British gardens. About 10 acres (4 hectares) in size, it is not enormously big, but it is still a garden which has many of the qualities which we all look for. It is really a series of gardens, each with something to give, and there are also excellent views beyond to which the eye is led by the two main vistas.

Hedges are a feature of this garden. They are well maintained and provide the visitor with ideas on how to position hedges.

Plants, though, are all-important and you can find a great variety of pinks and other *Caryophylacaea*, *Campanula latiloba* 'Hidcote Amethyst' sported at Hidcote, *Tropaeolum speciosum*, a climber with scarlet flowers, and *Hypericum patulum* 'Hidcote', the best of the St John's worts. Yuccas do well, as do tree paeonies. The ericaceous plants would not be happy here and it would be a struggle to grow them. If your garden soil is alkaline, do as the professionals do and grow something more suited to it.

NYMANS GARDEN

Handcross, West Sussex

Before the recent storm, the well-clothed look of Nymans was supplied by mature trees. Until replanting is complete, tree cover will be somewhat limited but there is still much to admire. Despite the fact the garden is divided into six sections, it is all one: it is easy to move through the garden from area to area without being aware you are changing emphasis. About 30 acres (12 hectares) in extent and with a lime-free soil, it is a joy to work, and almost the whole range of plants can be grown here. Because of the protection of the structure planting and of the walls, plants can be grown here which would not survive outside.

This is a garden where the planting is not intended just to provide cover, but where each plant has to pay its own way and stand on its own. There is a wealth of plant material for the visitor to consider. Tree cover is good and there are fine specimens of *Cryptomeria japonica*, *Torreya californica*, *Chamaecyparis lawsoniana* 'Wissellii' and *Libocedrus bidwillii*. Magnolia, aesculus, catalpa and quercus, though deciduous, provide good shade to the plants beneath during the summer.

In the open and sunny areas can be seen *Cornus kousa chinensis*, *Acer griseum*, *Eucryphia lucida*, *Camellia* 'Leonard Messel' and *Magnolia stellata*, which give height to the borders but which are flowering trees in their own right.

Nymans is a garden which begs more time on each visit.

SISSINGHURST CASTLE

Cranbrook, Kent

If an opinion poll asked which is the best-known garden in the country, I'm sure that Sissinghurst Castle would be very near the leader. It is smallish in area, being only 10 acres (4 hectares), but it's crammed full of all that is good in gardening. Although classed as lime-free, I am told there are pockets where it is possible to get a high pH reading.

In this garden for all seasons there is always something to see. In spring it is a mass of naturalised bulbs; there are also a rose garden, a cottage garden, a herb garden and the famous White Garden. A moat (now dry, which is just as well), surrounds the orchard.

Sissinghurst is, to me, controlled untidiness. It has that feel of being a cottage garden where plants do so well that they quickly take over the ground allotted to them and mesh with their neighbours.

Roses such as 'Cardinal de Richelieu', 'Fantin Latour' and 'Gloire de France' thrive with little attention. Climbers such as *Rosa longicuspis* and 'Madame Alfred Carrière' are profuse in growth and in flower. Cottage garden plants are the ones which catch the eye: lilies in many forms, aquilegias flowering from early in the season, euphorbias and tree paeonies adding colour of a diffrerent kind, whilst the day lilies go on throughout the summer. If it is a hardy perennial you are looking for, the chances are that you will find it somewhere in the garden: you just need time. Although Sissinghurst is loved by the connoisseur, it is equally good for the garden visitor.

TRESCO ABBEY GARDENS
Isles of Scilly, Cornwall

Tresco Abbey may only be reached by boat or air, but it is well worth taking the trouble to visit because it is almost like going to the tropics. Plants found in this garden are rarely seen anywhere else in the British Isles outside a heated greenhouse.

The planting to the windward side of the gardens is so dense and thick that it is almost impenetrable – an essential measure which helps provide the conditions necessary for plant growth. The Tresco Abbey plant list reads a little like *Who's Who*, as almost all the known genera can be found here. *Sparmannia africana* I grow in a 10in. (25cm) pot, but on Tresco it reaches 10ft (3m) in height! *Puya coerulea* produces its 8–9ft (2.4–2.75m) flower spikes in July; *Acacia dealbata*, the mimosa, grows like a weed and *Datura sanquinea* makes a plant 6ft (1.8m) high and more across.

Pelargoniums flower outside almost throughout the year, nestling close to garden walls; there are aeoniums from the Canary Islands and the large echium, which were so badly hit by frost this year, *Geranium canariense* with its anemone-like leaves about 4in. (10cm) across, and *Agave horrida* whose leaves are very sharply pointed.

Lonicera hildebrandiana reaches 15ft (4.5m) plus in growth and flowers profusely. *Kennedya nigricans*, an Australian climber with near-black flowers, and *Ipomoea learii* are two other unusuals to make a bright summer show.

WISLEY GARDENS

Wisley, Ripley, Surrey

In many ways Wisley is one of the most complete gardens to see. Laid out ornamentally, it is pleasing to stroll through whilst seeing a juxtaposition of plants ideally situated for garden use. Plants in this garden are all grown because they have a value and a position to fill, and each could be used in any garden which had the same requirements.

This is a garden where each month of the year there is something of interest, whether flower, foliage, fruit or bark. The size of the specimens is another point to take into account: how they might fit into your own garden may be discovered by observation here.

Plants cover the whole range from trees (and this includes the pinetum) to shrubs, perennials, annuals, fruit and vegetables. There are greenhouses on site as well as specialist gardens such as the rose garden, model fruit garden and vegetable garden, and there are the trial beds where new forms are tried in competition with their fellows.

Rhododendrons, azaleas, camellias, magnolias and lilies are massed in one section where there are hundreds of forms to select from. Plants such as *Sarcococca humilis*, *Fothergilla monticola*, *Halesia carolina*, *Sorbus mitchellii*, *Symplocos crataegoides*, *Amorpha lutescens*, *Magnolia kobus* and many more can be viewed under ideal conditions. *Narcissus cyclameneus*, *Cyclamen coum*, *Anemone nemorosa*, *Primula pulverulenta*, *Meconopsis betonicifolia*, *Incarvillea delavayi*, *Iris kaempferi* and *Astilbe arendsii* will perform over a long period to ensure that the garden has more than one tier of interest.

CHOOSING A GARDEN TO VISIT

There are literally hundreds of gardens that one can visit, from the great gardens of the National Trust which are open most of the year to very small cottage gardens that may be open on only one day a year.

The books below list these gardens and the times they are open.

Gardens of England and Wales Open to the Public. Published by the National Gardens Scheme.
Gardens Open Today. Published by Viking.
Gardens of the National Trust. Published by the National Trust and Weidenfeld and Nicolson, this lists the gardens run by the National Trust and includes a history of gardens and gardening.
A Celebration of English Gardens. Published by the English Tourist Board, this book provides details of 500 gardens to visit, plus information on hotels, special holidays, garden centres and nurseries.
Gardens to Visit. Published by Gardener's Sunday, 8 Mapstone Close, Glastonbury, Somerset.

SPECIALIST NURSERIES

Good garden centres have a great many plants in stock, but they are often only the well-known, rather ordinary varieties, so it is worth visiting specialist nurseries which have a range of the more unusual and interesting plants. If you cannot visit them, send for a catalogue.
Find the nursery or organisation specialising in the plant(s) you want in the list below, then turn to the alphabetical list on page 150 for the address.

Alpines
Amand, Jacques, Ltd
Blooms Nurseries plc
E.L.F. Plants
Iden Croft Herbs
Ingwersen, W.E.Th., Ltd
M. and R. Plants
Wells and Winter

Alstroemerias, dwarf hardy garden
Bailey, Steven, Ltd
Smith, P. J., Chantonbury Nursery

Annuals grown from seed
British Bedding Plant Association
Colegrave Seeds Ltd

Aquatic plants
Stapeley Water Gardens Ltd

Astilbes
Sealand Nurseries Ltd

Auriculas
Hyatt, Brenda, Auriculas

Azaleas
Crown Point Nursery
Hydon Nurseries Ltd
Knaphill Nursery Ltd
Starborough Nursery

Begonias
Blackmore and Langdon Ltd
Nielsen Plants Ltd

Bonsai
Bonsai Kai of London
Bourne Bridge Nurseries
British Bonsai Association
Bromage and Young Ltd
Glenside Bonsai
Herons Bonsai Nursery Ltd
Kai
Samlesbury Bonsai Nursery
Sei Yo Kan Bonsai
Tokonoma Bonsai Ltd

Bouvardia
Smith, P. J., Chantonbury Nursery

Bromeliads
Vesutor Ltd

Bulbous plants
Amand, Jacques, Ltd
Avon Bulbs
Bowlby, Rupert
Broadleigh Gardens
Four Seasons
Paradise Centre

Bulbs
Ingwersen, W.E.Th., Ltd
Van Tubergen UK Ltd

Butterfly-attracting plants
Iden Croft Herbs

Cacti
Abbey Brook Cactus Nursery
Holly Gate Cactus Nursery
Southfield Nurseries

Campanulas
Nielsen Plants Ltd

Carnations
Allwood Bros
Bailey, Steven, Ltd

Carnivorous plants
Carnivorous Plant Society
Marston Exotics

Chrysanthemums
Home Meadows Nursery Ltd
Tivey, P., and Sons
Woolman, H., (Dorridge) Ltd

Clematis
Fisk's Clematis Nursery

Conifers
Blooms Nurseries plc
E.L.F. Plants
Highfield Nurseries
Sherrards Garden Centre
Wells and Winter

Daffodils
Jefferson-Brown, Michael, Ltd

Dahlias
Bebbington, Tom, Dahlias
Home Meadows Nursery Ltd
Tivey, P., and Sons

Delphiniums
Blackmore and Langdon Ltd

Dicentra
Hardy Plant Society

Edible flowers
Iden Croft Herbs

Enkianthus
Hydon Nurseries Ltd

Ferns
Fibrex Nurseries Ltd
Highfield Nurseries

Foliage plants
Broadleigh Gardens
Ramparts Nurseries
Stydd Nursery

Fruit trees
Bowers, Chris, and Sons
Highfield Nurseries

Fuchsias
Castledyke Nurseries
Lockyer, C. S.
Oakleigh Nurseries
Oldbury Nurseries
Potash Nursery
Woolman, H., (Dorridge) Ltd

Gerberas
Bailey, Steven, Ltd

Ground-cover plants
Crown Point Nursery
Hillier Nurseries (Winchester) Ltd

Gypsophila
Smith, P. J., Chantonbury Nursery

Hanging baskets planted with annuals and perennials
Garden Centre Association

Hederas
Fibrex Nurseries Ltd

Herbaceous plants
Blooms Nurseries plc
Bowers, Chris, and Sons
Carlile's Hardy Plants
Chatto, Beth, Gardens
Four Seasons
Hardy Plant Society
Highfield Nurseries
Royal Parks Training Centre
Stydd Nursery
Vicarage Garden
West Country Plants

Herbs
Herb Society
Highfield Nurseries
Iden Croft Herbs
Wells and Winter

Hibiscus
Nielsen Plants Ltd

Hostas
Hydon Nurseries Ltd

Houseplants
Chessington Nurseries Ltd
Longmans Ltd

Hyacinths
Van Tubergen UK Ltd

Hydrangeas
Hever Castle Ltd

Ikebana flower arrangements
Ichiyo School of Ikebana

Irises
Broadleigh Gardens
Humphrey, V. H.
Kelways Nurseries

Lilies
Sealand Nurseries Ltd

Lupins
Woodfield Bros

Mediterranean plants
S.C.E.A. Pépinières Jean Rey

Narcissi
Van Tubergen UK Ltd

Old-fashioned plants
Plants from the Past

Orchids
British Orchid Council
Burnham Nurseries Ltd
McBeans Orchids Ltd
Orchid Society of Great Britain
Thames Valley Orchid Society
Wyld Court Orchids

Paeonies
Kelways Nurseries
Sealand Nurseries Ltd

Pansies
Bouts Cottage Nurseries
Hazeldene Nursery

Pelargoniums
A. P. Elite Plants
British and European Geranium Society
Fibrex Nurseries Ltd
Munro, Iris
Nielsen Plants Ltd
Oakleigh Nurseries
Thorp's Nurseries
Woolman, H., (Dorridge) Ltd

Peltatum
A. P. Elite Plants

Perennials
Hopleys Plants Ltd
M. and R. Plants
Notcutts Nurseries Ltd
Robinsons Hardy Plants
Rougham Hall Nurseries
Vicarage Garden

Pieris
Hydon Nurseries Ltd

Pinks
Allwood Bros
Bailey, Steven, Ltd
Ramparts Nurseries
Three Counties Nurseries

Pleiones
Butterfields Nursery

Polygonatums
Hardy Plant Society

Poppies, Iceland
Home Meadows Nursery Ltd
Rougham Hall Nurseries

Rhododendrons
Crown Point Nursery
Hydon Nurseries Ltd
Knaphill Nursery Ltd
Starborough Nursery

Roses
Austin, David, Roses
Beales, Peter, Roses
Cants of Colchester Ltd
Fryers Nurseries Ltd
Harkness, R., and Co. Ltd
Highfield Nurseries
Hillier Nurseries (Winchester) Ltd
Mattock, John, Ltd
Newberry, C., and Son Ltd
Nielsen Plants Ltd
Notcutts Nurseries Ltd
Rearsby Roses Ltd
Rosemary Roses
Sealand Nurseries Ltd
Stydd Nursery

Saintpaulias, streptocarpus and other *Gesneriaceae*
Clements, Tony, African Violet Centre

Shrubs
Blooms Nurseries plc
Bowers, Chris, and Sons
Burncoose and Southdown Nurseries
Crown Point Nursery
E.L.F. Plants
Four Seasons
Highfield Nurseries
Hillier Nurseries (Winchester) Ltd
Ingwersen, W.E.Th., Ltd
Notcutts Nurseries Ltd
Sherrards Garden Centre Ltd
Starborough Nursery

South African plants
National Botanic Gardens of South Africa

Strawberries
Muir, Ken

Succulents
Abbey Brook Cactus Nursery
Holly Gate Cactus Nursery
Southfield Nurseries

Sweet peas
Brackley, S. and N.

Trees
Burncoose and Southdown Nurseries
Crown Point Nursery
Hillier Nurseries (Winchester) Ltd
Notcutts Nurseries Ltd
Sherrards Garden Centre Ltd

Tropical plants
Anmore Tropical Botanic Gardens Ltd
Laurella

Tuberous plants
Paradise Centre

Tulips
Blom, Walter, and Son Ltd
Van Tubergen UK Ltd

Unusual plants
Bluebell Nursery

Vegetables
Marshall's Fen Bred Seeds

Venidio-arctotis
Allwood Bros

Violas
Bouts Cottage Nurseries
Cawthorne, R. G. M.
Hazeldene Nursery

Violettas
Cawthorne, R. G. M.

Waterlilies
Stapeley Water Gardens Ltd

Wild flowers
Chambers, John, Wild Flower Seeds

Xerophytes
Holly Gate Cactus Nursery

Zantedeschias
Fibrex Nurseries Ltd

The following is a list of nurseries and organisations which specialise in supplying particular types of plant(s), given in italics below the address.

A. P. Elite Plants,
A. P. Nursery, Vines Cross, Heathfield,
East Sussex.
Peltatum and zonal pelargoniums

Abbey Brook Cactus Nursery,
Old Hackney Lane,
Matlock,
Derbyshire.
Cacti and succulents

Allwood Bros,
Mill Nursery,
Hassocks,
West Sussex BN6 9NB.
Carnations, pinks and venidio-arctotis

Amand, Jacques, Ltd,
Clamphill, Stanmore,
Middlesex HA7 3JS.
Bulbous plants

Anmore Tropical Botanic Gardens Ltd,
Sir George Staunton Estate,
Petersfield Road,
Havant, Hampshire
PO9 5HB.
Tropical plants

Austin, David, Roses,
Bowling Green Lane,
Albrighton,
Wolverhampton
WV7 3HB.
Old-fashioned and climbing roses

Avon Bulbs,
Westwood, Bradford-on-Avon,
Wiltshire BA15 2AT.
Bulbous plants

Bailey, Steven, Ltd,
Eden Nurseries,
Silver Street, Sway,
Lymington,
Hampshire SO41 6ZA.
Carnations, pinks, gerberas, dwarf hardy garden alstroemerias

Beales, Peter, Roses,
London Road,
Attleborough,
Norfolk NR17 1AY.
Old-fashioned shrub and climbing roses

Bebbington, Tom, Dahlias,
Lady Gate Nursery,
47 The Green,
Diseworth, Nr Derby
DE7 2QN.
Dahlias

Blackmore and Langdon Ltd,
Stanton Nurseries,
Pensford,
Bristol.
Begonias and delphiniums

Blom, Walter, and Son Ltd,
Coombelands Nurseries,
Leavesden,
Watford,
Hertfordshire
WD2 7BH.
Tulips

Blooms Nurseries plc,
Bressingham Gardens,
Diss,
Norfolk IP22 2AB.
Shrubs, dwarf conifers, herbaceous plants and alpines

Bluebell Nursery,
Blackfordby,
Burton-upon-Trent,
Staffordshire.
Unusual plants

Bonsai Kai of London,
c/o 39 West Square,
London SE11 4SP.
Bonsai

Bourne Bridge Nurseries,
Oak Hill Road,
Stapleford Abbotts,
Romford, Essex
RM4 1JL.
Bonsai

Bouts Cottage Nurseries,
Bouts Lane,
Nr Inkberrow,
Worcestershire.
Violas and pansies

Bowers, Chris, and Sons,
Whispering Trees Nursery,
Wimbotsham, Norfolk
PE34 8QB.
Trained fruit trees, shrubs and herbaceous plants

Bowlby, Rupert,
Gatton, Reigate,
Surrey RH2 0TA.
Spring- and summer-flowering bulbous plants

Brackley, S. and N.,
117 Winslow Road,
Wingrave,
Aylesbury,
Buckinghamshire
HP22 4QB.
Sweet peas

British and European Geranium Society,
c/o 85 Sparrow Farm Road, Ewell,
Surrey KT37 2LP.
Regal and zonal pelargoniums

British Bedding Plant Association,
Agriculture House,
New London Road,
Chelmsford, Essex
CM2 0AP.
Annuals grown from seed

British Bonsai Association,
c/o Flat D,
15 St John's Park,
Blackheath, London
SE3 7TH.
Bonsai

British Orchid Council,
Church Bridge Lodge,
Batcombe,
Shepton Mallet,
Somerset BA4 6ER.
Orchids

Broadleigh Gardens,
Bishops Hull,
Taunton,
Somerset TA4 1AE.
Bulbous plants, foliage plants and Californian irises

Bromage and Young Ltd,
St Mary's Gardens,
Worplesdon,
Surrey GU3 3RS.
Bonsai

Burncoose and Southdown Nurseries,
Gwennap, Redruth,
Cornwall TR16 6BJ.
Trees, shrubs and ornamental plants

Burnham Nurseries Ltd,
Forches Cross,
Newton Abbott,
Devon TQ12 6PZ
in association with
Vacherot et Lecoufle,
B.P. No. 8,
30 Rue de Valenton,
94471 Boissy St Leger,
France.
Orchids

Butterfields Nursery,
Harvest Hill,
Bourne End,
Buckinghamshire
SL8 5JJ.
Pleiones

Cants of Colchester Ltd,
Agriculture House,
305 Mile End Road,
Colchester, Essex
CO4 5EB.
Roses

Carlile's Hardy Plants,
Twyford, Reading,
Berkshire RG10 9PU.
Herbaceous plants

Carnivorous Plant Society,
c/o 24 Osborne Road,
Brentwood,
Essex CM15 9LE.
Carnivorous plants

Castledyke Nurseries,
Castledyke Bank,
Wildmore,
New York,
Lincolnshire LN4 4XF.
Fuchsias

Cawthorne, R. G. M.,
Lower Daltons Nursery,
Swanley Village,
Swanley, Kent
BR8 7NU.
Violas, violettas and viola species

Chambers, John,
Wild Flower Seeds,
15 Westleigh Road,
Barton Seagrave,
Kettering,
Northamptonshire
NN15 5AJ.
Wild flowers

Chatto, Beth, Gardens,
Elmstead Market,
Colchester,
Essex CO7 7DB.
Hardy herbaceous perennial plants for dry and damp conditions

Chessington Nurseries Ltd,
Leatherhead Road,
Chessington, Surrey.
Houseplants

Clements, Tony,
African Violet Centre,
Station Road,
Terrington St Clement,
King's Lynn,
Norfolk PE34 4PL.
Saintpaulias, streptocarpus and other Gesneriaceae

Colegrave Seeds Ltd,
West Adderbury,
Banbury,
Oxfordshire
OX17 3EY.
Annuals grown from seed

Crown Point Nursery,
Ightham,
Nr Sevenoaks,
Kent TN15 0HB.
Rhododendrons, azaleas, shrubs, trees and ground-cover plants

E.L.F. Plants,
Cramden Nursery,
Harborough Road North,
Northampton.
Dwarf and slow-growing shrubs and conifers and alpine plants

Fibrex Nurseries Ltd,
Honeybourne Road,
Pebworth,
Nr Stratford-on-Avon,
Warwickshire.
Pelargoniums, hederas, ferns and zantedeschias

Fisk's Clematis Nursery,
Westleton,
Saxmundham,
Suffolk IP17 3AJ.
Clematis

Four Seasons,
Hillhouse Farm,
Cheney's Lane,
Forncett St Mary,
Norwich,
Norfolk NR16 1JT.
Shrubs, herbaceous and bulbous plants

Fryers Nurseries Ltd,
Knutsford, Cheshire.
Roses

Garden Centre Association, The,
19 High Street, Theale,
Reading, Berkshire
RG7 5AH.
Hanging baskets planted with annuals and perennials

Glenside Bonsai,
22 Water Lane,
Totton,
Southampton,
Hampshire SO4 3DP.
Bonsai

Hardy Plant Society,
The
214 Ruxley Lane,
West Ewell,
Surrey KT17 9EU.
Dicentra, polygonatum, bergenia and other hardy herbaceous plants

Harkness, R., and Co. Ltd,
The Rose Garden,
Hitchin, Hertfordshire.
Roses

Hazeldene Nursery,
Dean Street,
East Farleigh,
Maidstone, Kent
ME15 0PS.
Pansies and violas

Herb Society, The,
77 Great Peter Street,
London SW1P 2EZ.
Herbs

Herons Bonsai Nursery Ltd,
Wiremill Lane,
Newchapel,
Near Lingfield, Surrey
RH7 6HJ.
Bonsai

Hever Castle Ltd,
Edenbridge, Kent
TN8 7NG.
Hydrangeas

Highfield Nurseries,
Whitminster,
Gloucester GL2 7PL.
Conifers, ferns, fruit trees, herbaceous plants, herbs, roses and shrubs

Hillier Nurseries (Winchester) Ltd,
Ampfield House,
Ampfield,
Near Romsey,
Hampshire SO51 9PA.
Trees, shrubs, ground-cover plants and roses

Holly Gate Cactus Nursery,
Ashington,
West Sussex
RH20 3BA.
Cacti, succulents and xerophytes

Home Meadows Nursery Ltd,
Top Street,
Martlesham,
Woodbridge,
Suffolk IP12 4RD.
Bedding plants, chrysanthemums, dahlias, hardy plants and Iceland poppies

Hopleys Plants Ltd,
Much Hadham,
Hertfordshire
SG10 6BU.
Hardy and half-hardy perennials

Humphrey, V. H.,
8 Howbeck Road,
Arnold,
Nottingham
NG5 8AD.
Irises

Hyatt, Brenda,
Auriculas,
1 Toddington Crescent,
Bluebell Hill,
Nr Chatham, Kent
ME5 9QT.
Auriculas

Hydon Nurseries Ltd,
Clock Barn Lane,
Hydon Heath,
Godalming, Surrey
GU8 4AZ.
Rhododendrons, azaleas, enkianthus, pieris and hostas

Ichiyo School of Ikebana,
c/o Cherry Trees,
Providence Way,
Waterbeach,
Cambridgeshire
CG5 5QJ.
Ikebana flower arrangements

Iden Croft Herbs,
Frittenden Road,
Staplehurst,
Kent TN12 0DH.
Edible flowers and herbs, plants which attract butterflies and bees, and alpine plants

Ingwersen, W.E.Th., Ltd,
Birch Farm Nursery,
Gravetye,
East Grinstead,
West Sussex
RH19 4LE.
Alpine plants, dwarf shrubs and bulbs

Jefferson-Brown, Michael, Ltd,
Broadgate, Weston Hills, Spalding,
Lincolnshire PE12 6DQ.
Daffodils

Kai,
91 St John's Wood Terrace,
London NW8 6PY.
Bonsai

Kelways Nurseries,
Barrymore, Langport,
Somerset.
Paeonies and irises

Knaphill Nursery Ltd,
Barrs Lane,
Lower Knaphill,
Woking, Surrey
GU21 2JW.
Rhododendrons, azaleas and associated plants

Laurella,
c/o 26 Briton Crescent,
Sanderstead, Surrey
CR2 0JF.
Tropical plants

Lockyer, C. S.,
Lansbury,
70 Henfield Road,
Coalpit Heath,
Bristol BS17 2UZ.
Fuchsias

Longmans Ltd,
16 Holborn Viaduct,
London EC1.
House and conservatory plants, royal wedding bouquets

M. and R. Plants,
73 Cecil Avenue,
Hornchurch,
Essex RM11 2NA.
Alpines and hardy perennials

Marshall's Fen Bred Seeds,
Regal Road, Wisbech,
Cambridgeshire
PE13 2RF.
Vegetables

Marston Exotics,
Hurst Lodge,
Martock, Somerset.
Carnivorous plants

Mattock, John, Ltd,
The Rose Nurseries,
Nuneham Courtenay,
Oxford OX9 9PY.
Roses

McBeans Orchids Ltd,
Cooksbridge, Lewes,
Sussex.
Orchids

Muir, Ken,
Honeypot Farm,
Rectory Road,
Weeley Heath,
Clacton-on-Sea,
Essex CO16 9BJ.
Strawberries

Munro, Iris,
Elrig, Cantray, Croy,
Inverness.
Pelargoniums

Newberry, C., and Son Ltd,
Bulls Green Nursery,
Knebworth,
Hertfordshire
SG3 6SA.
Garnette and miniature roses

Nielsen Plants Ltd,
Danecroft Nurseries,
Station Road,
Hellingly, Sussex
BN27 4EU.
Begonias, hibiscus, campanulas, pelargoniums and miniature roses

Notcutts Nurseries Ltd,
Woodbridge, Suffolk,
IP12 4AF.
Hardy flowering and ornamental trees and shrubs, shrub roses, conifers, perennial and half-hardy plants

Oakleigh Nurseries,
Monkwood, Alresford,
Hampshire SO24 0HB.
Fuchsias and pelargoniums

Oldbury Nurseries,
Brissenden Green,
Bethersden,
Kent TN26 3BJ.
Fuchsias

Orchid Society of Great Britain,
c/o 120 Crofton Road,
Orpington,
Kent BR6 2HZ.
Orchids

Paradise Centre,
Twinstead Road,
Lamarsh,
Nr Bures, Suffolk
CO8 5EX.
Bulbous and tuberous plants

Plants from the Past,
The Old House,
1 North Street,
Belhaven,
Dunbar EH42 1NU.
Old-fashioned plants

Potash Nursery,
Hawkwell, Hockley,
Essex SS5 4JY.
Fuchsias

Ramparts Nurseries,
Bakers Lane,
Braiswick,
Colchester, Essex
CO4 5BB.
Pinks and grey foliage plants

Rearsby Roses Ltd,
Melton Road, Rearsby,
Leicester LE7 8YP.
Roses

Robinsons Hardy Plants,
Greencourt Nurseries,
Crockenhill,
Swanley, Kent
BR8 8HD.
Dwarf and unusual perennials

Rosemary Roses,
The Nurseries, Toton,
Beeston,
Nottingham
NG9 5FH.
Roses

Rougham Hall Nurseries,
Rougham,
Bury St Edmunds,
Suffolk IP30 9LZ.
Iceland poppies and other spring-flowering perennials

Samlesbury Bonsai Nursery,
Potters Lane,
Samlesbury,
Preston, Lancashire
PR5 0UE.
Bonsai

S.C.E.A. Pépinières Jean Rey,
Chemin de Lira,
84200 Carpentras,
France.
Mediterranean plants

Sealand Nurseries Ltd,
Sealand, Chester
CH1 6BA.
Astilbes, paeonies, lilies and roses

Sei Yo Kan Bonsai,
Buttercup Cottage,
Corfe, Nr Taunton,
Somerset TA3 7BY.
Bonsai

Sherrards Garden Centre Ltd,
Wantage Road,
Donnington,
Newbury, Berkshire
RG16 9BE.
Trees, shrubs, conifers and hardy plants

Smith, P. J.,
Chantonbury Nursery, Rectory Lane,
Ashington,
West Sussex
RH20 3AS.
Hybrid alstromerias, bouvardia and gypsophila

South Africa, National Botanic Gardens of,
Kirstenbosch 7735,
South Africa.
Indigenous and other flowers and foliages of South Africa

Southfield Nurseries,
Louth Road,
Holton-le-Clay,
Grimsby,
South Humberside
DN36 5HL.
Cacti and succulents

Stapeley Water Gardens Ltd,
92 London Road,
Stapeley,
Nantwich, Cheshire
CW5 7LH.
Waterlilies and aquatic plants

Starborough Nursery,
Starborough Road,
Marsh Green,
Edenbridge, Kent
TN8 5RB.
Rare and unusual shrubs, rhododendrons and azaleas

Stydd Nursery,
Stonygate Lane,
Ribchester,
Nr Preston, Lancashire
PR3 3YN.
Roses, ornamental foliage and herbaceous plants

Thames Valley Orchid Society,
c/o 15 Weald Rise,
Tilehurst,
Reading, Berkshire
RG3 6XB.
Orchids

Thorp's Nurseries,
257 Finchampstead Road,
Wokingham, Berkshire
RG11 3JT.
Regal and zonal pelargoniums

Three Counties Nurseries,
Marshwood, Bridport,
Dorset.
Garden pinks

Tivey, P., and Sons,
28 Wanlip Road,
Syston, Nr Leicester.
Chrysanthemums and dahlias

Tokonoma Bonsai Ltd,
14 London Road,
Shenley, Radlett,
Hertfordshire
WD7 9EN.
Bonsai

Van Tubergen UK Ltd,
Oldfield Lane,
Wisbech,
Cambridgeshire
PE13 2RJ.
Tulips, narcissi, hyacinths and other spring- and summer-flowering bulbs

Vesutor Ltd,
Marringdean Road,
Billingshurst,
West Sussex
RH14 9EH.
Bromeliads

Vicarage Garden, The,
Carrington, Urmston,
Manchester M31 4AG.
Dwarf perennial and herbaceous plants

Wells and Winter,
Mere House,
Mereworth,
Maidstone, Kent
ME18 5NB.
Dwarf conifers, alpines and herbs

West Country Plants,
Maxdene, South Cary,
Castle Cary, Somerset.
Herbaceous plants

Woodfield Bros,
71 Townsend Road,
Tiddington,
Stratford-on-Avon,
Warwickshire
CV37 7DF.
Hybrid lupins

Woolman, H.,
(Dorridge) Ltd,
Grange Road,
Dorridge, Solihull,
West Midlands
B93 8QB.
Chrysanthemums, pelargoniums and fuchsias

Wyld Court Orchids,
Hampstead Norreys,
Newbury,
Berkshire RG1 6BT.
Orchids

SPECIALIST SOCIETIES

There is a society to represent nearly every facet of gardening, if you want to extend your knowledge of any particular specialism. Most of these societies organise lectures and visits, produce a magazine and brochures, and have plant and seed exchange schemes.

Alpine Garden Society,
Lye End Link,
St Johns,
Woking,
Surrey.
Tel: 048 62 69327

British Cactus and
Succulent Society,
16 Crabtree Road,
Botley,
Oxford.
Tel: 0865 248802

British Carnation Society,
3 Canberra Close,
Hornchurch,
Essex.
Tel: 04024 41789

British Gladiolus Society,
10 Sandbach Road,
Thurlwood,
Rode Heath,
Stoke-on-Trent.
Tel: 093 63 2530

British Iris Society,
43 Sea Lane,
Goring-by-Sea,
Worthing,
West Sussex.
Tel: 0903 41993

British Pelargonium Society,
c/o Flat 1,
44 Barncombe Avenue,
London SW2 3AZ.

Carnivorous Plant Society,
c/o 24 Osborne Road,
Brentwood,
Essex.

Cyclamen Society,
24 Westell Close,
Clothall Common,
Baldock,
Hertfordshire.
Tel: 0462 895095

Daffodil Society,
1 Dorset Cottages,
Birch Road,
Copford,
Colchester.
Tel: 0206 330008

Delphinium Society,
Mr V. A. Labati, Hon. Sec.,
143 Victoria Road,
Horley,
Surrey.

Hardy Plant Society,
214 Ruxley Lane,
West Ewell,
Surrey KT17 9EU.

Heather Society,
7 Rossley Close,
Highcliffe,
Christchurch,
Dorset.
Tel: 042 52 72191

Herb Society,
77 Great Peter Street,
London SW1P 2EZ.

International Camellia Society,
Acorns,
Chapel Lane,
Bransford,
Worcester.
Tel: 0886 32610

National Auricula and Primula Society,
55 Elizabeth Road,
Moseley,
Birmingham.

National Begonia Society,
3 Gladstone Road,
Dorridge,
Solihull,
West Midlands.
Tel: 056 45 6323

National Dahlia Society,
9a High Street,
Kingsthorpe,
Northampton
NN2 6QF.

National Sweet Pea Society,
Acacia Cottage,
Down Ampney,
Nr Cirencester,
Gloucestershire.
Tel: 0793 750385

Royal National Rose Society,
Chiswell Green Lane,
St Albans,
Hertfordshire.
Tel: 0727 50461

Saintpaulia and House-plant Society,
82 Rossmore Court,
Park Road,
London NW1 6XY.

USEFUL ADDRESSES

Soil Analysis

Camland Advisory and Analysis Service,
36 Regent Street,
Cambridge.
Tel: 0223 68780

Craig Soil Services,
10 Windermere Park,
Windermere,
Cumbria.
Tel: 096 62 2818

Sutherland Soils Services,
PO Box 3,
Dept B. Dornoch,
Sutherland.
Tel: 086 281 715

Organic Gardening
Henry Doubleday Research Association,
Ryton-on-Dunsmore,
Coventry CV8 3LG.

Soil Association,
86/88 Colston Street,
Bristol BS1 5BB.

Trees
Aboricultural Association,
Ampfield House,
Ampfield,
Nr Romsey,
Hampshire SO5 9PA.

Forestry Commission,
Forest Research Station,
Alice Holt Lodge,
Wrecclesham,
Farnham,
Surrey GU10 4LH.

Horticultural Research
Institute of Horticultural Research,
East Malling,
Maidstone,
Kent ME19 6BJ.

Other Useful Addresses
Disabled Gardeners' Club,
Mary Marlborough Lodge,
Nuffield Orthopaedic Centre,
Headington,
Oxford.

English Vineyards Association,
The Chief Executive,
38 West Park,
London SE9 4RH.

National Society of Allotment and Leisure Gardeners Ltd,
The Secretary,
Hunters Road,
Corby,
Northants NN17 1JE.

National Trust,
42 Queen Anne's Gate,
London SW1H 9AS.

Royal Horticultural Society,
80 Vincent Square,
London SW1.
Tel: 01 834 4333

FURTHER READING

The All Seasons Garden
John Kelly
(Windward)

The Expert Books
Dr D. G. Hessayon
(PBI Publications)

Gardening from Which?
(Monthly magazine)

Garden Plants for Connoisseurs
Roy Lancaster
(Unwin and Hyman)

Perennial Garden Plants or The Modern Florilegium
Graham Stuart Thomas
(Dent)

Reader's Digest Encyclopaedia of Garden Plants and Flowers
(Reader's Digest)

Successful Organic Gardening
Geoff Hamilton
(Dorling Kindersley)

INDEX